9

HOPE NATION

Edited by ROSE BROCK

HOPE

NATION

YA AUTHORS SHARE PERSONAL MOMENTS OF INSPIRATION

PHILOMEL BOOKS

PHILOMEL BOOKS
an imprint of Penguin Random House LLC
375 Hudson Street
New York, NY 10014

Library of Congress Cataloging-in-Publication Data is available upon request.

Printed in the United States of America.
ISBN 9781524741679
10 9 8 7 6 5 4 3 2 1
Design by Ellice M. Lee.
Text set in Perpetua.

For Madeleine, Olivia, Michael, and Mom,
who inspire me to start and end
each day with hope.

CONTENTS

ROSE BROCK

Introduction

Dear Reader,

Like some of you, I'm a reader. Like others, I wasn't always. My family came from Germany to the United States when I was in elementary school, and for all kinds of reasons, I struggled. Coming from somewhere different was hard. Learning English—learning *in* English—was hard. That slowly changed, thanks mostly to books. Books became my escape, my window to this new American world. I still remember my first book friendships; before I had real friends at my new school, I basked in the company of fictional friends. Since that point, reading books has been one of the things I cherish most.

Here's another thing you should know about me. Until she passed away, I was fed a steady diet of hopeful anecdotes by my immigrant mother. Hers were often focused on her childhood during World War II in Germany. After losing all their possessions in an Allied bombing, my grandmother and her five children fled their city to Bavaria to start over again while they waited for my grandfather to be released from a camp for prisoners of war. Although my family was on the wrong side of history, it seemed that the

HOPE

lessons served to my mom were ones that resonated, and for that reason, in my childhood home, finding hope was a directive. It was expected that the world's lemons would be made into fresh lemonade. Perhaps that is the reason I'm an optimist. A dreamer. A hoper. And whether it's in my genetic makeup to see the glass as half full or it's a product of conditioning, I love stories of resilience and tenacity, and I look for hopeful stories everywhere—in books, in movies, and most importantly, in real life. The older I get, the more I understand that finding and holding on to hope can be hard. At times it can feel impossible.

So what is *Hope Nation*? Simply, it's a collection of unique and personal experiences shared by some of my favorite writers for teens. Stories of resilience, resistance, hardship, loss, love, tenacity, and acceptance—stories that prove that sometimes, hope can be found only on the other side of adversity. I'm so grateful to each of these talented writers for sharing their own paths to hope.

Mr. Rogers of *Mr. Rogers' Neighborhood* once said that during a crisis, it's vital to look for the helpers. The authors featured in *Hope Nation* are our helpers; the gift of their stories is the reason I am able to share this book with you. The making of it is a hopeful endeavor in every way—in lieu of being paid to share their stories, my amazing team of contributors have donated 100 percent of their fees to charities that give meaning to them, organizations and charities working to make our world a better place for you and me. And my publisher is matching each donation.

To me, *Hope Nation* is the gift I want to give back to all the young people in my life, especially my daughters, Madeleine and Olivia. It's for the teens closest to me who have been left feeling disempowered and hopeless. We see you. It's for all of you that we say, "Hope is a decision." I hope it's a choice you make for yourself.

Dr. Rose Brock
Grapevine, Texas
2018

DAVID LEVITHAN   LIBBA BRAY   ANGIE THOMAS
ALLY CONDIE   MARIE LU   JEFF ZENTNER
NICOLA YOON   KATE HART   GAYLE FORMAN
CHRISTINA DIAZ GONZALEZ   ATIA ABAWI
ALEX LONDON   HOWARD BRYANT   ALLY CARTER
ROMINA GARBER   RENÉE AHDIEH   AISHA SAEED
JENNY TORRES SANCHEZ   NIC STONE
JULIE MURPHY   I. W. GREGORIO   JAMES DASHNER
JASON REYNOLDS   BRENDAN KIELY

DAVID LEVITHAN

We

THIS IS WHAT I BELIEVE:

Despair comes from the things that are bigger than us.

Hope comes from the things that are our size.

This is where I'm coming from:

I don't know many truly bad people. In fact, when I try to think of a truly bad person in my life, I come up with a handful of selfish ones, a secondhand knowledge of a number of ignorant and/or misguided ones, and a painful dose of ones who hold opinions with which I passionately disagree. But the ones who would kick me when I was down? They are vastly outnumbered by the ones who would help me out.

I know I am lucky in this respect.

When I'm dealing with other people, especially strangers (and especially especially strangers who are walking slowly on the sidewalk or cutting me off with their cars), I often experience a profound annoyance, peppered with an occasional flash of genuine anger. But what's interesting to me is that underneath it all is an equally profound love. I operate under the assumption that any given person, if I got to know them, would be completely worthy of love and consideration and kindness. To know a person's story is inevitably to understand their humanity and feel a loving kinship with them, no matter how different the two of you may seem at first.

This love, this understanding of humanity, is what gives me hope.

You see:

When push comes to shove, most people will help.

When push comes to shove, most people will aspire to decency.

When push comes to shove, most people want the center to hold.

I genuinely believe this.

So.

The despair comes when individuals unite into power structures that distance them from this humanity. In the blindness of the mob, or the government, or the corporation, or the armed forces, there can be a strange and dangerous impulse to cut moral corners. Any situation that allows us to dehumanize others is asking for trouble. It plays to the worst in us.

I hate this. I hate that the value of a human life can ever be seen as anything other than absolute and equal.

But look. Change happens when people stop looking at the bigger scale and start seeing things on the human scale. Or let's not just call it change—let's call it progress. I'm a gay Jew living in America at the start of the twenty-first century, which is inarguably the best time for a gay Jew to be living. Set anywhere else in history, I would be much more afraid of the grave, and much more certain to stay in the shadows. Not because people hated me, but because people hated my category. Which isn't to say that there aren't haters out there now. Oh, there are. But there are fewer of them. And there are fewer of them because people started seeing the category on the human scale . . . and realized that the people within it are just as human as they are. That's how progress works. And the fact that it does work (often at agonizingly slow speed) is what gives me hope.

In my life so far, I've come to count on the fact that whenever the forces of despair push at us, there is always counterbalance that comes from the forces of hope. I have seen it on a micro level—the way when a book is challenged, it will always be defended, most often on very human terms, for very human reasons. And I have seen it on a macro level—when a handful of terrorists caused such devastation in New York City on 9/11, there was an outpouring of millions upon millions of people who responded with care and love and kindness. Most recently, after the election of 2016 and the inauguration of Donald Trump, we saw the remarkable way people came together to protest—and we've since seen that protest sustained. The things his government is doing make me despair. The reaction to it makes me hope.

Which leads me to this story.

It's fiction, but it's not really fiction. On Inauguration Day in 2017, I was attending the American Library Association convention in Atlanta, Georgia, and marched with two librarian friends in a bigger group of librarians, teachers, authors, and publishers in a much bigger group of protesters in the streets of Atlanta. Every year I write a story for my friends for Valentine's Day, and in 2017 the protest was still very much on my mind when I sat down to write the story. So I made some characters do what I did and see what I saw. Which is why I feel comfortable sharing it in a collection of essays—sometimes we fiction writers need to make up a story to tell a truth of the moment. And this certainly holds the truth, to me, of that day. And that truth still translates for me, months later, into hope.

WE

(the Valentine's Day story, 2017)

"I BET THIS WOULD BE a great place to pick up girls," Courtney says to me, her eyes scanning the hundreds of pussy hats pouring by Coca-Cola World on the way to the march.

"If you say so," I tell her. The only girls I ever pick up are friends like Courtney, who can bring a lesbian reality check to my flightier gay-boy fancies.

"I've already given my heart away, like, five times," Courtney tells me. "They just haven't noticed yet."

"They're distracted by your sign."

"No doubt."

There's pretty strong competition for best sign here. Since we're in Georgia, there are a lot of creative suggestions for how to put the *peach* into *impeach*. (It helps that the president's skin is the same color as a nectarine's.) There's an umbrella with an angry cat face on it that threatens "This Pussy Grabs Back." Another sign has Keith Haring figures spelling out "Make America Gay Again."

Courtney went full-Bechdel with her poster art, cartooning famous queer women in various protest poses. Gertrude and Alice hold hands and stand their ground. Frida wears a shirt that says, "I'm Kahling You Out." Sweet Ellen pumps a fist and calls out, "Nasty If I Wanna Be!" Audre grins and holds a sign that reads, "The Lorde is on our side, and that is all we need." Sappho gets a speech bubble and defiantly proclaims, "I will turn your lies into fragments!"

The problem is, it's starting to rain, and although other people laminated their signs or covered them with clear tape, Courtney's is entirely unprotected.

"Shit," she says as a few drops start to make Susan Sontag's hair streak.

I fumble open my umbrella as the spatter turns into a torrent. It's not big enough to cover us both. People duck into doorways for cover; we hug the Coca-Cola World entrance, but it gives us only a partial respite.

People continue to hurry toward the plaza outside the Center for Human and Civil Rights, where the march is set to begin. I worry that if we delay too long, we'll end up missing the speeches, including John Lewis's kickoff. He's the person we all want to see.

Courtney stares down at her poster. I know she spent a lot of time making it.

"I guess I'll keep it under my coat for now," she says. She's wearing a pink jacket that will barely cover the poster board.

"Don't do that," a girl next to us says. She looks like she could be Alice Walker's teenage self, and she's put down her own tape-covered sign, which reads, "'We have been raised to fear the yes within ourselves'—Audre Lorde."

"I like your quote," Courtney says.

"Thanks," the girl responds as she rummages through her bag. "Ah, here." She plucks out a translucent square. "Take this."

Emergency Poncho, the label reads.

"It's see-through," the girl explains. "So people can still see that kick-ass sign."

"Don't you need it?" Courtney asks.

The girl gestures to her own yellow raincoat. "I'm covered."

"But does this really count as an *emergency*?" I ask. "What if this poncho is meant to save a life?"

Courtney, whom I've known for years, shoots me the look she deploys when something that falls out of my mouth gets relegated to Attempted Quip status without crossing the Effective Quip threshold.

The amusing part is that the girl I've known for only a minute or two shoots me the exact same look. Since both of them are shooting at me, they don't even notice their identicalism.

"Thank you," Courtney says, breaking away from me to look back at the girl. "I'm Courtney. This is Otis."

"With an *O*," I chime in. (It's just something I do.)

"I'm CK," the girl offers.

"Well, thank you, *CK*," Courtney says with some enjoyment.

"Hey! Courtney's initials are CK!" I realize aloud. "Your name doesn't happen to be Courtney Khan, does it?"

I see something shimmer across CK's face, but she quickly shakes her head. "Nope. CK stands in for my first and middle names— don't ask, 'cause I'm not going to tell. My last name is Hamilton."

As soon as she says this, three people behind her start squeeing and saying how much they LOVE *Hamilton*. "I'm not throwing away my shot!" they sing. Others join in.

"You must get that a lot," I say to CK.

"You have no idea," she replies.

"Well, boys named Evan Hansen must have it worse," I point out. "They must wake up and curse Ben Platt on a daily basis."

Instead of getting a big laugh, this observation is greeted with a sheet of water that comes crashing to the ground.

"Well, that's not good," Courtney says. She unfolds the emergency poncho and attempts to put it on. The head hole is not immediately discernible from the armholes. CK hands her protest sign over for me to hold, then helps Courtney straighten the poncho out.

"You're an EPT, aren't you?" I ask.

Both Courtney and CK stare at me.

"What?" I say. "An EPT—get it? Emergency poncho technician?"

They start laughing. But it's not at my joke. I can tell.

CK looks at Courtney. "He doesn't have a clue, does he?"

Courtney looks at me like I'm a pug. "Nope."

But . . . okay. Now they're next to each other. Getting along. So at least I've done *something* right.

"Are you here with a group?" I ask.

"I am," CK says. "But we seem to have scattered. I was going to try to find them."

There's a beat. I wait for Courtney to say it, since it would be better for Courtney to say it. But I also know that crushes tend to tie Courtney's tongue, so I step into the pause.

"Want to march with us for now? It would be great to have an EPT on hand. Just in case something malfunctions."

"Otis! Stop!" Courtney says. Then quickly she turns to CK and adds, "I mean, with the acronym. Not with the invitation. You should totally march with us."

"I'd love to," CK says, taking her sign back from me. "Shall we?"

"Into the rain!" I say.

"Into the rain!" Courtney and CK echo.

The rain is falling too fast to sink into the ground, so the sidewalk is a mess of puddles as we join the throng heading to the plaza. And it *is* a throng now, a convergence. It feels like people are coming from all corners of the state to be a part of this. All ages, all races, big groups and individuals walking on their own. And the weird part is, none of them seem like strangers. We all have the fact that we're here in common, and that's enough to feel a deep and inspiring kinship. It's been a rough two months since Election

Day; we've had to question a lot of things we never thought we'd have to question, and the whole time we've had to worry that we're more alone in our anger and sadness than we thought we'd be. It was a national election, but it felt so *personal* too—profoundly personal. When the breakage of the country occurred, it felt like we'd been broken as well. Now it feels like the pieces are coming back together. On the outside and on the inside. Just from gathering together and carrying signs and walking as one.

Plus, there are the hats. I taught myself how to knit in order to create my hat and Courtney's. They didn't come out quite as well as the YouTube tutorial promised they would. They *are* pink yarn creations with two cat ears each—but these particular cats are strays that have been in a few territorial fights, leading to a certain patchiness of fur and waywardness of ear.

CK's hat, though, is up to my grandmother's standards for knitwear. It's stitch-perfect, its ears poised and alert. As she and Courtney get a few steps ahead of me, I see she's even knit herself a tail, which mischievously pokes out of her yellow slicker.

I wonder if Courtney's noticed it yet. She seems more intent on focusing on every word CK says.

The crowd is starting to coalesce around us, so that by the time we round the corner to get to the plaza, it's a solid sea of people, and the only way to go any farther would be to bob and weave, leaving a trail of "excuse me"s in our wake.

I've made it back to Courtney and CK's side, but it's as if my umbrella is really an invisibility cloak for all I'm registered by their rapport.

"... my father actually used the phrase *Communist hordes*, while my mother cloaked her disapproval in terms of my own safety," Courtney is saying. "'What if there's a bomb?' she actually asked. And I couldn't help it—I said, 'Well, why don't you tell your side not to bomb us, okay?' That really pissed my dad off—he said we were just playing into the enemy's hands—and I had to ask, 'Who *exactly* are the enemies, Dad? You did get the memo that Republicans love Russians now, right? So is it ISIS? Do you think ISIS is going to target the Women's March in Atlanta?'"

"What did he say to that?" CK asks.

"My mother interrupted at that point, to say she only wanted me to be safe. And I said if my safety was really her number one concern, then maybe she should have voted to make sure I'd have health care after I graduated . . . and luckily that's when Otis honked and I was out of there. To give her credit, there's been some follow-through—she texts every ten minutes to make sure I'm fine."

"My mom's marching in Washington," CK says. "She lives up there. And I keep texting her every ten minutes, to make sure she's fine."

"I think our biggest threat right now is pneumonia," I say. The wind has joined the rain, rendering my umbrella's future precarious.

"I'm sorry I don't have any more emergency ponchos," CK tells me.

"How about a comforter?" I ask. "Do you happen to have a water-proof comforter in there?"

It's nearly one o'clock, which is the time the rally is supposed to start. But now some people are saying it's been delayed because of the rain. I try to check the website, but my phone can't get any Internet—there are too many people using the signal at once.

"It doesn't make any sense to delay," Courtney says. "We're all here."

We hear a cheer—but it's coming from behind us, not from the plaza. We turn and see a parade of six or seven people zigzagging through the crowd. They're all holding the same sign—a photo of Carrie Fisher as Princess Leia, staring down the enemy with her hands calmly behind her neck.

"We are the resistance," the caption on the posters reads in bold Barbara Kruger letters.

All the other posters—"Fight Like a Girl," "F-ck This Sh-t," "Women's Rights Are Human Rights," "Our Lives Begin to End the Day We Become Silent About Things That Matter"—part to let the Princesses pass.

"That's what I'm talking about," CK says, saluting.

"Can you feel it?" Courtney asks.

"What?"

"The Force. It's here."

It takes CK a second to realize that Courtney is making a joke *and* completely serious. Because even though it's not the return of any Jedi, there's definitely a Force unleashed here, the same Force that rises any time you strike back against an empire. I think we all like to believe that Carrie Fisher would approve.

I notice that CK isn't making any attempt to find her friends in the crowd. Possibly because it would be futile—there are just too many of us. But possibly because she's finding Courtney's company enough.

Since I know Courtney so well, I can see what CK's attention is doing to her. She hasn't expected it—she never expects it—and as a result she's not quite sure what to do with it. The two pieces are clearly clicking together, but it has yet to be determined what the full shape of the puzzle is. All that can be known for sure is the click. Courtney's been brokenhearted before, so she can't help but feel the pain of the unclicking buried inside that initial click. But she *can* choose to ignore it, if she's convinced enough.

All of this can be read in her face, in her posture. All of this can be read, if you know how to read her.

We're close to the "Make America Gay Again" banner again, and I can't help but check out who's carrying it. One is a muscled guy in a muscle T-shirt that reads, "I blocked Mike Pence on Grindr and this is his revenge." Another is a woman who looks like she could be a teacher in any elementary school classroom in America, wearing a dress that would make Ms. Frizzle proud, covered in stars and planets.

As the rain continues and the wait goes on, there's some shifting from foot to foot and more checking of phones. Every now and then, there's a chant—"Rise up! Rise up!" and "This is what democracy looks like!"—but by and large, the feeling that pervades is . . . patience. In the context of a crowd, I find this somewhat remarkable. We, who are always in a rush, who always have more than a dozen things we need to do by the end of the day—we are okay with standing still. We are fine with talking to each other until it's time to go. It's as if the strength of the congregation has briefly turned down the volume of our obsession with time. This gives me hope; we have not only the power of our voices, but the power of patience on our side.

Courtney, CK, and I are lucky we're on the sidewalk; the people on the grass are beginning to sink into it, although they don't seem to mind too much.

When Courtney's poster folds a little under her poncho, CK reaches over to smooth it out.

"Thank you," Courtney says. And I notice that CK doesn't step back—she remains close. Courtney stays there too. Even in the rain, even in the crowd, Courtney looks happy. And I think this is the first time in a while that I've seen that. We've had our guard so far up about what's happening to our country that I think it's made it harder for us to let our guard down in our daily lives. Especially Courtney. I can believe in dancing my despair away, in singing loud even when your heart is dying. But not her. She won't risk coming out of her shell, because she feels she needs to be in her shell to survive.

She stayed over with me on Election Night, because as the dumbfounding results unfolded, we both knew there was no way she'd be going back home to face her parents. *This isn't happening*, we kept saying to each other, and although I found it funny that the newscasters seemed as gobsmacked as we were, Courtney couldn't find anything funny about it. Funny had moved off to another planet. Exiled.

The morning after the election was like emerging from a dark, dark room into the glare of a spotlight. It was a shock so strong that I couldn't walk steady, couldn't make out shapes or colors. My thoughts were a startled cacophony of causes and effects, and no matter how quickly I blinked, I couldn't sort them out, couldn't get my eyes to adjust. In my sadness, I reached out. In my fury and my incomprehension, I reached out. And Courtney was there, just as I'd hoped she would be.

But even as I reached out, I could feel she wasn't reaching back—not as much. She was retreating.

She might have disappeared altogether, into sleepless worry and unyielding despair. But I wouldn't let her. I forced her out to movies. I went over every Saturday night to watch *SNL*. I rallied her around this march. I certainly understood the desire to pull back into a shell, to protect yourself from all the venom that suddenly filled the air. But I also felt that as safe as a shell may be, it also prevents you from moving, from uniting, from resisting in an active way. Trump and Bannon and all the other assholes wanted us inside our shells so our voices would never reach them, would be heard only by our own ears. I just wasn't going to let them win like that. And Courtney—well, Courtney took some coaxing. But this march gave her a reason to step out of the shell.

There's a roar from the plaza—the speeches are beginning. Unfortunately, the loudspeakers sound like they're underwater— we can discern voices, but not words. We can sense we're being welcomed by speaker after speaker—that's the tone. But as ten, then fifteen minutes pass, there's a certain amount of restlessness brewing. It's still raining, but not as much. Side conversations continue.

Then, all of a sudden, there's a cheer much louder than any of the ones before. *JohnLewisJohnLewisJohnLewis,* the crowd around us buzzes. "We love you, John!" people call out. We can feel him stepping to the podium, even though we can't see it.

The loudspeakers find a divine burst of energy and lift to loudness. Or maybe it's just that all of us fall into an absolute, reverent silence. Whereas the other speakers were clouds of voice, intimations of tone, John Lewis's words round the corners and travel the lengths of the avenues. They are faint, but they are present. They persist.

"Sometimes you have to turn things upside down instead of right side up," he tells us. His voice bears the weight of the trouble he's seen, and his words soar on the strength of the victories he's shared. "When you see something that is not right, not fair, not just, you have a moral obligation, a mission, and a mandate to say something, to do something. We cannot afford to be silent now. I just want to say thank you. You look so good! This is unbelievable. There's hundreds and thousands of people, I tell you! I want to thank you for standing up, for speaking up, for getting in the way, for getting in trouble, good trouble, *necessary* trouble."

The crowd erupts into a chant of *"Thank you, John! Thank you, John! Thank you, John!"* Courtney, CK, and I all chant along.

Congressman Lewis says, "Thank *you*. Thank *you*. You're wonderful." Someone must cry out "I love you," because he comes back with "I love you too. I love you so much. You'll never know how much I love you."

It's almost childish how purely this affects me. Here we are, in 2017, and it's still stunning and moving to me to hear a grown man talk about love so openly, so unashamedly.

I notice a guy about my age who's leaning into an older group of protesters. They can't hear what's coming over the loudspeakers, so as Lewis's words take shape, the young man repeats them to the group.

"You don't need to use social media," he tells them. "Use your feet. Use your hands." A few seconds after the rest of us, they cheer.

Courtney reaches out and takes my hand. Then she takes CK's hand and holds it, too.

"I know something about marching," Congressman Lewis tells us. "I know something about marching. When I was much younger, had all of my hair, and was a few pounds lighter, I marched in Nashville . . . I marched in Washington . . . I marched from Selma to Montgomery. I'm ready to march again! I come here to tell you—don't let anybody, *anybody* turn you around. And never, ever, *ever* give up hope. Never lose hope."

We cheer some more. For him. For hope.

We barely feel the rain. I only feel Courtney's hand in mine, and sense CK's hand in hers.

"We're fighting for our sisters, for our mothers, for our daughters. We're also fighting for our brothers, for our sons, for those who are not able to stand up and fight for themselves."

As I look at the multitudes around us, we are told that there are gatherings in cities across the nation just like ours, that there are more than half a million people right now in Washington, DC, alone. And it's as if I can feel the alchemy of hope working, that transmutation of despair into determination.

Lewis concludes with a rousing proclamation. "I'm fired up and ready to march! I have on my marching shoes! So let's do it!"

What does it feel like to hear your voice join tens of thousands of other voices in a wordless cry of pride and defiance? It feels like somehow you have attained a state of nature. It feels like your strength, which you have long limited to your body's capacity for strength, now transcends that body and takes on the shape of a storm. You do not lose yourself—even in the enormity, you still hear your own voice the loudest, and those that are close to you are still distinct. But you are yourself and something much larger than yourself, all at once.

CK reaches her free hand back to me, and I take it. The circuit is completed.

"This is amazing," she says. "This is everything we need."

Courtney and I agree. I am the first to let go, but the two of them remain connected. I lean over to see if the marching has begun. It's going to take a while for the movement to get to us—there are some people already hankering to go, but I figure it'll happen when it happens. There are more cheers from the front of the crowd—Congressman Lewis and the others must be on their way forward.

I look at more of the signs: "We Shall Overcomb." "John Lewis Represents Me, Trump Doesn't." "Build Bridges, Not Walls." I look at more of the people carrying the signs: Teenagers with their parents. A group of older ladies who look like they just got off the tour bus on their way to see the Eiffel Tower, fanny packs prominent. Two men who can't stop kissing each other. The rain has definitely ended, so the umbrellas have been folded and the pink hats are again the most prominent marker of our spirit. "I'm Really Not Happy About This." "Keep Your Tiny Hands Off Our Press." "WE the People. Stronger."

The sun comes out, and almost immediately it feels warmer. CK takes off her raincoat and folds it around her tail, then looks at Courtney and says, "Here, let me help you out of that." She reaches under the poncho and lifts both sides so it clears Courtney's poster, then floats above her arms. Courtney gives in to the movement, holds her head straight so CK can lift the poncho free. For a moment they stand there, CK's arms above them both, Courtney's arms at her side, their faces inches apart.

"Thank you," Courtney murmurs.

"Glad to be of some use," CK replies, crumpling the poncho down so it becomes no bigger than a small plastic bag.

They couldn't be like this in any crowd. But in this crowd, the intensity between them can emanate. Nobody else will question it or interfere with it. The moment gets to be itself.

Slowly, we begin to move. I'm not sure I've ever seen a more polite crowd. There's a lot of "You first—no, *you* first," and eventually we are moving around the Georgia Aquarium and making our way to the plaza.

CK reaches into her pocket and takes out her phone. I'm hoping it's because she wants to use the camera, but no—instead she's checking a text. Then another.

As much as Courtney may think she's hiding it well, I can see the concern on her face. The needle of bad luck is pressing hard against the balloon of her happiness. She was starting to think of CK's time as hers, but now she's feeling like she was only borrowing it from CK's *real* friends, out in the crowd.

True friend that I am, all I can think is *Please may she not already have a girlfriend. Please may she not already have a girlfriend.*

"What's up?" I ask casually as she texts a response.

"Nothing." CK puts the phone back in her pocket. "Some of my friends are over there." She points to a building that has yellow construction-material walls. There have to be tens of thousands of people between here and there. "They want me to find them. But I was like, *That's just not gonna happen.*"

"It's okay if you need to go," Courtney says. Because that's what Courtney does—always provides the escape route from her own heart. I try to signal her to stop, to not give the out unless she wants it taken.

"I'm really good here," CK says. "Assuming you guys don't mind."

"It wouldn't be the same without you," Courtney quickly replies. And I think, *Good for you. Don't worry about where it ends up; just keep it going.*

We're coming onto the plaza outside the Center for Human and Civil Rights now, and nearing the new sculpture that lies at its heart. The crowd could easily go around it, but most of us are going through. The sky is lighter now, the weather beginning to feel like early summer, and volunteers are handing out free bottles of water for anyone who needs them. As we walk under the monument, Margaret Mead's quote plays against the glass, backed by white clouds and more than a hint of light blue sky.

NEVER DOUBT
THAT A SMALL
GROUP OF
THOUGHTFUL,
COMMITTED
CITIZENS
CAN CHANGE
THE WORLD.

It's as if Mead is speaking to us across time. I stop to take a picture, already sensing that I'm going to need to collect moments from this day to get me through the next four years.

Pockets of people cheer at Courtney's sign and CK's sign. They hold them up proudly. People start to chant, "Hate does not make America great!" getting louder and louder with each repetition. We get to the stairs by the side of Coca-Cola World, and as we're walking up, I turn around to see what I think will be a trail of people behind me . . . and instead find people for as far as the eye can see. Pink hats and baseball caps. The full skin spectrum. "The future is STILL female," and "I'm with HER. And HER. And HER. And HER. And HER," and "White Silence Is Violence. Black Lives Matter," and "All People Are Created Equal." Behind me, a woman in a black Windbreaker holds a portrait of Ruth Bader Ginsburg saying "I Dissent." We aren't just marching through the plaza—we are surrounding it.

"Our Bodies. Our Minds. Our Power."

Everyone is waiting her turn to march—and then everyone is *taking* her turn to march.

We skirt around Coca-Cola World. As we stride, the city watches over us. We find our way to Centennial Drive, which is now the main artery of the protest. We enter the bloodstream.

Courtney and CK are ahead of me again, are holding hands again, and from the way they lean in to each other, I can construct the rough shape of a heart. Next to me is a white girl who looks about twelve years old, wearing a white T-shirt with a similar red heart on it; she wears red lipstick, and her hair looks like it was shaped by 1920s Hollywood. She isn't carrying a sign; she is enough of a sign herself, walking purposefully with her mother beside her.

I fall a little farther back. The woman beside me is carrying a Hillary sign. In front of me there's a dark-skinned toddler on one of his moms' shoulders—a black-and-white-striped long-sleeve shirt underneath his orange tee. He looks fussy, so his mom turns around and walks backward so he can face his other mom, who makes faces to cheer him up. He bursts into a cloud-break grin, facing us all now like he's conducting the crowd. Everyone around him welcomes this.

"Choose Love"

"If you're not ANGRY, you're not paying ATTENTION"

"Ctrl Alt-Right Delete"

"Women Made Me Who I Am"

"We Belong"

"Injustice Anywhere Is a Threat to Justice Everywhere"

"#loveislove"

I spot a row of portable toilets and see a bespectacled guy with a bright pink Radical Queer Librarians poster. As I pass, a blond spitfire of a librarian joins him. I've noticed many librarian-related signs in the crowd today, although I can't explain why. I am happy to be librarian-adjacent.

I catch up to CK and Courtney, who are now talking about the largest crowds they've ever been part of . . . which turns into a conversation about the first concerts they ever went to . . . which turns into a conversation about whether an affection for the Jonas Brothers is more or less shameful than an affection for Nelly. (The answer, of course, is that neither is particularly shameful.) Courtney starts to serenade CK with "Burning Up." CK responds with "Just a Dream." We're passing the convention center (more librarians, cheering from the sidewalk) and getting close to the modernist monolith of the new stadium, which in its construction phase looks like something Darth Vader deemed too ugly for his own backyard.

We're heading for the elevated length of MLK Boulevard, and as we turn onto it, a brass band a few dozen feet ahead of us starts to play. I don't recognize the song at first, but then the tune kicks in and I realize it's "I'm Every Woman." Courtney and a few other women in the crowd start to sing along. But CK, for the first time, looks *bashful*. I don't get it, but as the song goes on and the bashfulness persists, my gaytuition kicks in—in my case, it's most useful for making largely useless pop culture connections.

"Holy shit!" I say to her, far too excited. "Your real name is Chaka Khan, isn't it?"

Courtney, thinking I'm making a dumb joke, groans, "*Otis.*" Then she turns to CK and says, "Sorry about him. He was raised by goats."

"No," CK says. "Actually, he's right. My mom is . . . a big fan."

"No shit!" Courtney says.

"Mmm-hmm," CK confirms.

"Well then, dude, you *have to* sing," Courtney says, pulling at her arm.

"After all, it's all in you," I add.

"Shut up," CK and Courtney say at once, then sing along as the four tubas at the center of the brass band bring the tune home.

As we walk across the bridge made by the boulevard, we can see that the line of people continues long past where we were by the convention center. It could be ten thousand people, it could be a hundred thousand—after a certain point, it's hard for the mind to map, since we're so far beyond the realm of counting.

"This is what democracy looks like!" we call out again and again as we continue down MLK. I can hear waves of cheers coming from ahead—when we get closer to the spot where the cheers are emanating from, I realize that the crowd is cheering the police officers who are watching over us. People are calling out thanks, and many of the police officers are smiling and waving back.

There are no protesters in sight.

My phone vibrates, and I see it's a message from my mom,

checking to see if everything is okay. As I'm texting her back, I look at Courtney and say, "Hey, text your mom." She turns to CK and says the same thing. CK then turns to the woman next to her and says, "Text your mom." The woman says it to the guy next to her. And then, all of a sudden, people are starting to chant, "Text. Your. Mom! Text. Your. Mom!" People are pulling their phones out, taking pictures, sending them. I take a video for my mom of the chant, then send it to her with the message *You did this. We're all good.*

As we get to the edge of the Fulton County Courthouse, there's an African American woman standing on a ledge above the sidewalk. She looks like she, too, could be a librarian—glasses, cool earrings, white T-shirt, black skirt. She is hoisting a sign above her head in a way that reminds me of that famous shot of Sally Field in *Norma Rae*. It proclaims, "I Am My Ancestors' Wildest Dreams." We call our admiration out to her, and she calls us forward.

The brass band pipes up with "This Land Is Your Land." Behind them, another sign is hoisted: "Protect Each Other."

I turn around and face two women with matching "Be a Good Human" sweatshirts. Behind them, the streets are filled to the horizon line.

"Repro rights, not rape culture"

"You're Not Putin Your Hands on This Pussy"

"Unite with love. Resist with love"

And beyond that, behind other signs, I can only make out words.

"Love—"

"Same—"

"Black—"

"Justice—"

"History—"

There are rainbow flags. Star Wars caps. More and more pink hats of every shape and size.

It is a sea of people, and I feel that one of the strengths of this is that it not only joins us to the other bodies of humanity that are forming in cities and towns across the world today, but reaches back and unites us with all the other marches in history that were about justice and fairness and resistance to those who would undermine equality and opportunity. It's as if when we march today, we are retroactively marching behind John Lewis in the sixties and marching on the mall for gay rights and abortion rights in the nineties and marching to protest the war in Iraq in the first decade of this century and the brutality in Ferguson only a short time ago. All of these histories overlap in us, and they are the fuel to our fire.

We are nearing the state capitol, the end of our route. We have by now been out here for hours, and our feet are starting to feel sore. But it doesn't feel like enough, not nearly enough.

The capitol is in view now. The band unexpectedly fills the air with "I'll Fly Away," and we all start to sing along. People who learned it from their parents or their grandparents. People who learned it from church. People who learned it from Alison Krauss. People who learned it from George Jones or Johnny Cash. We sing it at the capitol and then past the capitol, right up to the heavens.

I'll fly away, Oh Glory
I'll fly away in the morning.
When I die, Hallelujah, by and by
I'll fly away.

As I watch, Courtney puts her arm around CK's shoulders. CK

reaches over and takes off Courtney's hat. Then she reaches to her own hat, removes it, and places it on Courtney's head. Next, she puts Courtney's on her own head. They sing the whole time.

We strangers are all smiling at one another. We are so much louder together than we are on our own. I knew I was here to protest; I knew I was here to unite. But what I didn't know was that I was here to remember why I am so in love with the world. As hard as it is, as difficult as it may be, I am deeply, unfathomably in love with the world that can have us here like this. I will always fear losing this world, but I must always keep in my heart what having it is like, and what loving it can bring. I must remember that I am not the only one who loves it. This love is shared by multitudes. It is visible in tens of thousands of different ways right now. Because when you are in love with the world, you want the world to know it.

There is a sniper on the roof of the capitol, watching over us. When we wave to him, he awkwardly waves back. John Lewis is probably on his way to a reception by now, or on his way home. This isn't a race; there is no finish line. There is simply a corner where some people are going one way and some people are going another.

I'll fly away

I'll fly away

We cheer as the band ends the song, because music is a victory, and our march is a victory, and we love each other so much at this moment, all of us in this together.

I don't want to breathe this in—breath passes through too quickly.

I don't want to simply remember it—memory starts to feel unreal.

I want this in my DNA.

I suspect it's always been in our DNA.

As we reach Capitol Avenue, we need to make way for all the marchers behind us. When we get to the corner, I will ask CK which direction she needs to go. When she says left, I'll say I need to go right—and then tell Courtney I'll catch up with her later, so they can continue their conversation wherever it may go. I will watch them walk away in their matching-yet-different pink hats, and then I will wander through the city as we marchers continue on, the glory remaining in our hearts. *Were you there?* we'll ask each other. *I was there,* we'll say. From this center, we will spread to the far reaches, go to our homes and to the places less welcome to us. We will not stop being together. Our love will endure.

DAVID LEVITHAN **LIBBA BRAY** ANGIE THOMAS
ALLY CONDIE MARIE LU JEFF ZENTNER
NICOLA YOON KATE HART GAYLE FORMAN
CHRISTINA DIAZ GONZALEZ ATIA ABAWI
ALEX LONDON HOWARD BRYANT ALLY CARTER
ROMINA GARBER RENÉE AHDIEH AISHA SAEED
JENNY TORRES SANCHEZ NIC STONE
JULIE MURPHY I. W. GREGORIO JAMES DASHNER
JASON REYNOLDS BRENDAN KIELY

LIBBA BRAY

Before and After

IT'S A SCOWLING JUNE MORNING, and the threat of rain weights my skin and sits on the back of my tongue with a metallic tang. I have plans to go to the Holiday Inn pool with my best friend, EJ, later in the day, and I'm hoping the rain will move through quickly, like it often does on summer days across the plains of North Texas. My precollege summer stretches out before me in mental, sun-drenched Polaroids of joyful freedom. I am eighteen. Nothing lingers. Nothing is permanent.

Three weeks ago, I graduated from Denton High School, class of 1982. On my chest of drawers is a photograph of me in my purple-and-gold cap and gown, a pair of saddle Oxfords and ankle socks poking out below the hem instead of the heels my mother would've preferred. I'm posing beside my racing-green Toyota Corolla sports car with its stick shift that makes me feel like James Bond with every thrust into the next gear. It's beautiful and small and quick. My brother has put in a kick-ass stereo and speakers, and I'm just pretentious enough to announce to every boy who cops a ride with me, "The speakers? Yeah, they're *Bose*" as some sort of cool-chick mating call. There's no AC, but if you roll down both windows and drive fast, the wind does the job fine. There are seat belts too, of course.

But who needs those?

I'm up early to give my father a ride to the DFW airport. He's got a business trip to Connecticut, and now that I'm a big bad graduate, I'm responsible enough to make the twenty-five-mile drive to DFW and back. My mother has started her litany of Things I Must Do, but I barely hear. I'm thinking about the pool and my hopes that this will be the summer my pale, freckled skin finally achieves that elusive golden glow that makes EJ's legs look so good in shorts. It's the reason I can be talked into slathering myself in baby oil and iodine, the mixture shaken to a cosmetic pink in the Johnson's bottle, then lying on a towel-draped pool chair under a take-no-prisoners sun for hours until I burn and flake and freckle anew. EJ and I will go to the pool later, after the rain. We'll listen to Queen albums in the cool dark of her house, which will be empty as always. Her father travels constantly, and her mother abandoned EJ and her little sister six months after my parents divorced and my father moved to Dallas with his secret lover, John, the step-father I am not supposed to tell anyone about for safety reasons. Or she and I might go into Dallas to flip through albums at Sound Warehouse on Lemmon Avenue, where the employees—a mix of Jesus-bearded hippies and spiky-haired, skinny-pants-wearing New Wavers—make us feel flirty and giddy. Maybe we'll go to one of our small town's three movie theaters, even though we've seen every movie out. We could walk the mall. Grab a dipped cone from the DQ. Some of our friends are still in town and not away on last family vacations before college. Come dusk, we could all trek out to Hog Valley and sit on the trestle bridge listening to Black Sabbath, telling ghost stories while we wait for a possible glimpse of our terrifying local legend, the Pigman, rumored to be a murderous half-man, half-pig "wereswine" possessed by the devil himself.

The real action in our town doesn't happen until after dark, though, when anybody with a driver's license races up and down University Drive, a.k.a. "The Strip," looking for a date, for a party, for a fight, for something to remind them they're young and alive. But that's not really our crowd. We wouldn't be caught dead cruising with all the jocks and socialites . . . on purpose. I mean, if it happens accidentally, sure, fine. "We're just driving, not cruising," we'd surely sneer, and turn up AC/DC's "Highway to Hell" as loud as the radio could go. Then I'd punch the gas, shifting rapidly—first, second, third gear—as we'd squeal down the long flat of asphalt toward the distant rise of I-35, the highway that crosses our huge state from the Rio Grande Valley to the plains of Oklahoma.

But we've done all that before. We're itchy for something different. We are nowhere, wanting to be *somewhere*, idling at the starting line of adulthood. I'm impatient for it. I'm impatient for the life I've daydreamed about—boys, college, theater, travel, new adventures, maybe true love—to begin. That's why I love driving and the freedom it offers. Rambling across country roads past sunburned fields populated by cattle and bluebonnets and the occasional faded windmill gives me space to think and dream. With each drive, I test myself to go farther from home and toward independence.

"You ready?" my dad asks as I finish up the last of my Sara Lee butter pound cake.

I will never eat Sara Lee butter pound cake again. I won't even be able to tolerate the smell of it.

I smile and grab my car keys. "Yep."

And then the two of us are on the road, a trip that will forever divide my life into a "before" and "after."

"You're doing a great job," my father tells me, and I puff up inside. Competency feels good. Feels grown-up. I want so much all the time, but I'm unfocused, my considerable energy everywhere at once, like a sprinkler on high. My teachers often chided me, "You've got so much potential. But you've got to take things seriously." It's not that I don't take things seriously. If anything, in the heart that I hide from most everyone, I take things *too* seriously. I want so much. I dream of being an actress or a comedienne, like my favorites, Gilda Radner and Bette Midler. I'm insecure, though. Especially about my looks. Most of my friends have already had sex. I'm the last virgin standing. My older brother, not known for his boundaries, has regaled me with unvarnished tales of his sexual exploits, and I can see and hear from what he and his friends talk about that how a girl looks is everything to them, which is disheartening, terrifying, and infuriating. How will I ever be enough? How will I ever *stay* enough?

I've convinced myself that the only way I'll ever be sure I won't be discarded like my mother is if I'm perfect. On the surface, I'm funny, sarcastic. But underneath, I work impossibly hard at not letting any cracks show. I'm terrified of my own vulnerability. I keep it at bay with jokes most of the time and silence the rest, lost to daydreams and doodling and the never-ending hope that I will prove my teachers right about that potential, that I will find a boy who loves me and thinks me beautiful. That I will believe myself to be beautiful. That I will not spend the rest of my life working so hard at being perfect in order to feel I have the right to take up space. In college, I tell myself, things will be different. In college, my real life will begin.

The trip to the airport is a piece of cake. I drop my father at the terminal, wave goodbye, then navigate the morning rush-hour traffic back home. Even with the windows open, the air's tight. I shouldn't have worn my long-sleeved Tom Petty and the Heartbreakers T-shirt, but I love that shirt. I bought it at the concert a few weeks ago, and it makes me feel cool. Being a "cool girl" is on my "being perfect" checklist. Stalled in traffic, I glimpse my reflection in the rearview mirror. In those fleeting seconds before I can pick myself apart, I think I'm pretty. There are the almond-shaped, blue-gray eyes that read green in the bright sun. The emergence of cheekbones. A strong, straight nose—on the prominent side like my Irish-lineage grandmother's and dusted with freckles. The pouty bottom lip that I like to imagine is inherited from my French great-great-grandmother. She was pretty, they tell me.

The rain's starting as I take the exit ramp from I-35 back into Denton. I've got both hands on the wheel as I sing along to the radio. "L.A. Woman" by The Doors. Jim Morrison's psychedelic, menacing croon blasts from my kick-ass Bose speakers. I'm approaching the intersection of Dallas Drive and Teasley Lane. If I turn left down Teasley, I can drive to our former neighborhood, past our old house with the bay-windowed breakfast nook where I used to sit to sketch. After the divorce, my parents had to sell that house, and now my mom and I live in a small town house with a faulty foundation on the other side of town on a street of oil-stained driveways and chain-link fences and a Baptist church whose summer marquee reads, "If you think it's hot now, don't die without Jesus."

The rain comes harder, slickening the road. At the intersection, the traffic light slides to warning-yellow, but I'm going too fast to brake. I decide to sail under the light before it hits red. So I press the gas. In the left-turn lane opposite, a white pickup truck has other ideas. At the last second, it shoots in front of me. My foot hits the brake hard. The tires slide sideways as my car hydroplanes on the glass-like pavement and swerves into a violent spin. I am trapped inside the tornado, the landscape a blur. I have to stop, but I don't know how, and I'm terrified. There's a grassy median. If I can make it to the grass, I might find traction there. But it's hard to see while spinning out of control. I angle toward it and hope for the best. *So fast, so fast. Which gear will stop me?*

In the chaos, my foot slips to the gas.

The last thing I see is a giant steel light pole coming straight for me.

When your car hits a giant stationary object at forty miles an hour, the impact is tremendous. The front of your car—hood, bumper, engine, carburetor—crumples in on itself like an empty Coke can squished between two strong palms. Your body, fragile, all-too-human, travels forward like a projectile, especially if there's no protective seat belt to hold it back. Witness it in slow motion, and you see the car's collapsing front end shoving the steering wheel upward as you fly forward. If the steering wheel hits an inch above your eyebrows, you'll be dead instantly. If it hits an inch lower, at your throat? Dead. The best hope is that your face takes the brunt of the impact, bones crushing, flesh tearing, muscles, tendons, and nerves severed into a spaghetti squash of uselessness. That's the best scenario. The one that lets you live. Lucky you.

Back at the crash now. Watch as your face hits the steering wheel with the impact of a jet-propelled battering ram, so hard it breaks the wheel off at its column. (Goodbye, Irish nose. So long, baby cheekbones. Good to know you, lips.) You merge with the shattered steel and hard plastic like a dying Transformer that can't quite transform. It is not clear just yet whether you really are one of the lucky ones. You are not awake. You are not there. You have always longed to be elsewhere.

Now you are.

That thing they tell you about your life playing out before your eyes? True. While I'm unconscious in the smoking, sputtering ruin of that Toyota, mine spools backward like the home movies my parents threaded onto our old projector. The memories are hazy-bright, slightly glitchy, and without context, a randomly tossed handful of moments presented sans meaning. But the feeling is good. I am not unhappy. And then, as if extracted roughly from a warm memory cocoon through a scratchy tunnel of sound, I'm coming to inside my mangled car. The radio still plays. It's too loud. I want it off. Around me are muffled voices, approaching sirens. The voices sound worried. Panicked. One shouts, "She's moving! She's awake!"

"Sweetheart, can you hear me?"

"Yes," I say, and gag on blood. *Is that* my *blood?*

A sense of disassociation floods through me, complete with a kindly robo-calm narrator for all my misfiring thoughts: *The car has stopped spinning. Oh. Good. That's good. I had an accident. Mom will be mad. She worries too much. They'll have to clean me up before I can go onstage tonight. So much blood. My head hurts. Makeup will cover it for the show tonight. Yes, makeup. No. Wait. That play is over. Oh, good. Okay. Turn off the radio. Turn it off.*

Shock is an amazing survival mechanism. This is how it works, like a photographer trying to distract a crying toddler with a succession of toys: "Don't feel the pain in your broken bones. Don't panic because you're having trouble breathing. Don't know how close you are to real danger, to death. Just act like it's all normal." Shock serves its purpose, and I am riding on some high-grade shock here. The panicked people with their sirens are debating how to get me out of the mangled car that has its steel arms wrapped tightly around me.

"I can get out," I say. "I just need to turn off the radio. It'll run down the battery."

Normal. All normal. Thank you, Shock. You are a most excellent companion.

"We'll do that for you, honey," say the Panicked People.

"Oh. Thank you."

They want to put me on a stretcher, but I remember something.

While soaking in my grandmother's claw-foot tub at her house in the hills of West Virginia and pawing through her *Reader's Digest*, I came across a story about a boy who died from a bike accident. No one had thought to turn him on his side, and he choked to death from a bloody nose.

"I'll walk," I say.

Opening my eyes is impossible for some strange reason. "I can't see," I say, and hands hold gently to my arms, guiding me to an ambulance. With the first steps, a sudden, sharp betrayal of pain sneaks past my good buddy Shock and shoots up both legs. "I think I broke something," I say in my new robo-voice. I am placed on a gurney and rushed to our local hospital a mile away, where emergency room doctors and nurses bustle around me, fast and decisive, firing off questions:

"Can you open your right eye?"

I do. Pain pinballs against the bones of my skull. "Yes. It hurts."

"Can you see?"

"Yes."

The doctor exhales. "Good."

I don't know why this matters so much, but he said *good*, so that must mean everything is okay. Of course everything will be okay. I'm eighteen. My future is unwritten. Nothing is permanent. Rain moves through. Rain moves away. Sun comes out again in time for the pool.

"We're going to have to cut off your clothes to examine you," a nurse's voice says.

"But it's my concert T-shirt," I say, as if this is explanation enough.

"I don't think we can get your shirt off over your head."

"I can do it," I insist. I'm a distance runner. Very strong. No sweat. I try to sit up. Try to move my arms. Any part of my body. Impossible. For the first time, Fear nudges Shock out of the way.

The nurse: "We need to cut off your clothes, honey."

"Okay," I say in a small voice. The scissors make a terrible rasping sound as they tear through my blood-soaked clothes and the concert T-shirt I bought with my own money.

My mother has arrived. It's a small town, and a message has reached her at Texas Woman's University, where she is working on her master's degree. She moves into the room now, asking questions in her English teacher way, a dry-eyed crisis warrior, an Appalachian mountain girl turned Texas matriarch. I feel bad that she's alone. My mother and I fight a lot. I tell her she's too controlling, too overprotective. I want her protection just now, but I'm also afraid she'll never let me drive again. My family doctor is here. He's been my family doctor since I was a tomboyish ten-year-old. He has watched me grow up. Seeing me now, he cries softly. I can hear his strangled voice: "We need to get her to Dallas immediately."

Quickly, they load me into an ambulance, my mother following in her car. As we scream down the road, sirens blaring, I'm hideously embarrassed. So much fuss. So silly. I'll be fine. When I was fifteen, the doctors thought I had cancer in my leg. I spent a week in the hospital as they ran all sorts of tests, and in the end, the tumor was benign. See? Fine. Everything's fine. I'll be fine. I'm just very sleepy is all. So, so sleepy. An exhaustion I never felt in my years of cross-country runs overtakes me. And all that blood rushing down into my stomach has me nauseated as hell. Up front, the EMT speaks softly to the driver: "Are we going to lose her?"

I will not go to sleep.

At Dallas Presbyterian, my injuries are explained to me in clinical terms by trained voices. I have been in an accident. Do I remember what happened? *Yes: Rain. Brake. Spinning. Pole. Radio too loud. Ouch.* Do I know what day it is? *June twenty-first.* Do I know who's president? *Reagan.* Am I having trouble breathing? *Yes. Very much yes.* Blood and mucus coagulate in my throat till at times I fear I will suffocate. This is because I don't have much of a nose left. The impact of the steering wheel against my face has obliterated the breathing apparatus pretty good. I've also fractured my jaw, which eventually will need to be set and wired shut, but they don't dare do that yet because I need to be able to try to breathe through my broken mouth and to throw up, if necessary. The ER doc has opted not to perform a tracheotomy. Instead, someone I cannot see will periodically suction the choking, bloody mucus from my throat when it gets really bad, which, it turns out, is pretty often. "You're lucky to be alive," they tell me in a refrain I'll come to hear a lot. *Lucky* is an empty word. It does not stand on its own, but is dependent upon its relative position for meaning: *You're lucky . . . that tiger ate only your brother. You're lucky . . . you didn't take that boat ride that killed a hundred other people. You're lucky . . . to only lose your whole face and not be dead.* Luck is not the same thing as hope.

There are other injuries—the right leg and left foot, crushed cheekbones, broken teeth, bruised sternum and ribs. But the big one is the left eye. It's injured somehow. I don't know how; no one really tells me. Just "injured" is all the information I'm given. Shock is starting to come off duty, and Pain is just punching the clock for its long shift. They want to give me pain meds but can't just yet. First, there's got to be exploratory surgery to stabilize me and make sure I don't have any internal injuries that are bleeding out. There's no time to waste. A mask comes down over my face and I'm unconscious.

I am in surgery for nine and a half hours.

I wake in a drugged panic, still intubated. I can't see, can't talk, can't beg them to take out the gag-inducing tube. And I know one thing: I'm going to puke. My hands grasp and clutch desperately in an effort to signal my distress. I tug at the tube. Oh God, I'm choking to death. Hands push mine down.

"Hold on. Hold on, sweetheart," an anonymous voice says.

I *can't* hold on. I will choke on the puke and the plastic in my throat. I've never been more terrified or powerless. In the nick of time, someone removes the tube.

I sit up and vomit Sara Lee butter pound cake everywhere.

Somewhere in the sky, my father's plane travels unbothered across the country. It won't land for another four or five hours. When it does, a group of sober-faced ministers from the Presbyterian General Assembly will gather around him in the anodyne airport among shoeshine stands and luggage retailers. Softly, they'll deliver the bad news and escort him to a different gate to wait for another plane that will bring him straight back to Texas. He will take that trip numb and mute, pleading silently with God. Bargaining with God. Furious with God. My father is a forgiving man, but it will take him decades to forgive God and himself for asking me to make the trip in the first place. His path to hope is years away and will come in a surprising way. Seven years into the future, he will be diagnosed with HIV. Six years after that, it will progress to AIDS. In those years of his death sentence, he will get sober, adopt a cat, foster animals, write editorials against corruption and abuse of power, enjoy his grandchildren, sing in a chorus, play the church organ, raise money for an orphanage, and retire to the mountains of northern Colorado. As he lies dying in hospice listening to Judy Collins singing "Amazing Grace," he will tell me that he sees grace and beauty in everything, that everything will be okay. He will liberate himself from shame. He will stop whittling himself down in a futile quest to make himself suitable for those who told him that being gay is a sin. He will know he is loved. He will finally love himself.

He will die in the arms of hope.

For now, while my father takes his agonizing journey back to me, my mother has called the person she needs: John. It's a *Modern Family* moment a good thirty years before *Modern Family* exists. My mother links hands with her gay ex-husband's new partner, the two of them holding each other up during the long bedside vigil. For a brief, conscious moment, I hear my mother's voice in one ear, John's in the other, both of them letting me know they are near. And finally, my father is there too, and my three parents arrange themselves into a new, hopeful form of love. Sometimes, hope is rearranging. It is making more room than you thought possible.

A few days into my two-week hospital stay, the surgeon, Dr. Broderick, stops by. He chats amiably with my parents and me.

He's British, and I love hearing his *Masterpiece Theater*—worthy accent. "I'm going to shine a light in your left eye," he says at last in his plummy tones. "Let me know when you can see it." I wait. And wait. And wait. My sinking stomach knows the truth first. Surely by now he's flashed that light at my eye.

"Did you see it yet?" he asks.

"No," I answer, hoping it doesn't mean what, deep down, I know it means. Denial is also not hope, though it's often confused for it. Denial is holding fast to a rope not tethered to a supporting beam, then closing your eyes as you fall. If you keep your eyes closed, you might not see hope approaching. It can be small. Small as a moment. Small as a hand reaching for yours once you let go of what you can no longer afford to keep clutching.

Dr. Broderick clears his throat. The seconds stretch. "Right," he says, businesslike. "Here's the truth. Your eye has been damaged beyond repair. You may choose to keep it, of course, but it will be unsightly, and it may become infected and infect the other eye, risking blindness. Or we can remove it and fit you with a prosthesis, a glass eye, which will look like the other one." My father is upset. I can hear his terse, lowered voice in the room, though I can't quite make out his words. I only hear Dr. Broderick's response: "She's an adult now. It has to be her decision."

I am finally an adult, just like I wanted. This is the first adult decision of my life: allowing doctors to remove my eye and fit me with a prosthesis. Permanent. Irrevocable. Forever and ever, no take-backs, amen. In the end, it isn't much of a choice, but it's still mine to make.

I tell them to take it out.

. . .

"So there's good news and there's bad news," my mother says the next day when they come to wheel me into surgery again. "The bad news is, you lost your contact lens. The good news is, they don't think you'll need it anymore." I laugh. Oh God, do I laugh. My mother laughs too. Great whooping, cackling laughter. The hospital staff is horrified, but there's so much hope in a laugh. My mother pats my hand. And then I'm wheeled back into the operating room.

Every four hours, I'm allowed a shot of morphine. For the first two hours, I waft in and out of a twilight sleep inhabited by beeping machine sounds and muffled announcements from the nurses' station, and wild, fantastical fever dreams in which I'm never quite sure whether I am awake or asleep. The borders of reality have been erased. All is porous. The second two hours are another story. Morphine has its limits. During the grit-it-out time, the pain is a living animal clawing me up inside. The twilight sleep becomes a nightmare landscape in which I am utterly alone, an isolation so complete I wonder if this is madness. Opening my eyes brings stabbing pain, so I never open my eyes unless instructed to do so. The breathing is half suffocation, and the suctioning brings only temporary relief. Between that and the drugs, my two-week stay in the hospital is a bit like being in a sensory deprivation chamber.

The nurses at Dallas Presbyterian Hospital are incredible, though. There is my savior, a redheaded nurse with an Irish brogue who comes marching in with scissors when the clueless oral surgeon repositions my broken jaw slowly over a day using braces and rubber bands—a misguided attempt that causes excruciating, electric pain to shoot up through my head if I move so much as a millimeter. "That child hasn't cried the entire time she's been here. He must be killing her!" she says, cutting through the industrial-strength rubber bands and forcing the doctor to come in on a weekend to wire my jaw shut and stop the pain for good. The head nurse, Karen, is a saint—sweet voiced and reassuring, always checking on me. It is only later that I learn that her teenage stepdaughter was killed months earlier. A car accident. And there is my beloved Randy Trawnik, the incredible ocularist with the wicked sense of humor who will make all my prosthetic eyes for years, painstakingly crafting them first out of wax, then out of plastic, painting the color to match just so, creating the illusion of blood vessels using tiny bits of red embroidery thread, thin as candy floss. He has a prosthesis himself, from having accidentally shot his eye out when he was also eighteen, and I'm grateful to have a friend and advocate all wrapped up in a compassionate, skilled artist who truly gets it.

There is only one person I could do without. On my last day in the hospital, a dark-haired, pinched-mouthed nurse comes in to open my curtains and take my vitals. As she squeezes my wrist between her fingers to check my pulse, she reprimands me for being so upbeat all the time. "You need to stop that. You're going to have to deal with these feelings, you know." It registers like a slap. At this moment, I have no idea what lies ahead, no idea about the years of surgeries—the bone and cartilage grafts taken from ribs and ears, the attempts to reconfigure my eye socket and nose again and again. I'm just grateful to still be alive. Whether she "means well" (the most damning of sentences) or is a sadistic bitch doesn't matter. Whatever her motivations, she has no right to tell me how to feel, what to feel, and when I need to feel it. That is mine alone to determine. I say this less to condemn her and more to tell you that *you* have a right to arrive at your feelings in your own way and in your own time, and that's nobody's business but yours and, if needed, a trained therapist's. (And even there, you are still in control of that particular feelings bus.) So, we'll leave it at "she meant well but should have kept her mouth shut."

The bandages come off. I'm handed a mirror. The last time I'd seen myself was a glimpse in the rearview mirror of my car when I'd thought, in that fleeting moment, that I was pretty. It's oddly fascinating to view my swollen, sutured face. Like seeing somebody else's. Our faces are part of our identities, and this part of my identity has now been altered forever. There are stitches keeping my top lip together. Braces and wires holding my jaw shut. A permanently lopsided smile thanks to severed nerves. There's a temporary nose, flat as a pancake. And a sunken hollow where my left eye used to be. A clear conformer—a piece of plastic—holds the shape until I can be fitted for a prosthesis in two months' time. The nurses tape an eye patch on me and help me to a wheelchair. We hug goodbye. And I go home to heal.

That summer, nothing seems real or permanent just yet. I'm still hopeful that I'll be "fixed." I go to countless doctors' appointments. People come to visit. They tell me that I'm strong. So strong. *Really, really* strong. And because they say it enough, I feel that I've got to *be* that strong girl. I sense the unspoken message swimming under their words: *Don't be sad or angry. There's nothing worse than a sad or angry misshapen girl. No one wants to be around that.* My mother spends her summer having to take care of me—putting all my food into a blender, helping me into and out of the tub, cleaning the wounds I can't reach. It's a tremendous strain on her, I know. "I guess I'm just not supposed to go back to school and get my master's!" she says angrily one day in frustration. And I get it even as I absorb the guilt.

In August, my jaw is unwired. The cast comes off my leg. And I'm fitted for my first prosthesis. That's when reality slinks in and sits down hard. I don't know what I expected. That's a lie. I do know. I expected that everything would be just like before. The prosthesis would magically work, like Steve Austin's bionic eye on the show *The Six Million Dollar Man*. On TV, everything works out. But my new eye is nothing like that. The crash obliterated not just my left eye but all the bones around it as well as the nerves that make an eye blink and track. The unmoving prosthesis sinks back deep into the damaged socket, and the baffled doctors can't figure out how to make it come forward in my face. It's no more than a painted rock stuck into the hole where I used to have an eye.

"Looks great. So realistic! I can't even tell," everyone says.

They're lying. I know they're lying, but I need them to lie. Besides, word on the street is that I'm strong and brave and not angry or sad, and I want to play my part like the good actress I am, like the actress I will never become. Actresses need working eyes, I tell myself. Only my mother says nothing. Because she is the most honest person I know.

Summer ends. With the exception of EJ, most of my friends leave for various colleges in far-flung cities. Numb, I pack up my clothes, books, records and record player, and, at the last minute, a little yellow journal, a graduation gift from the man who'd been fixing my mother's roof at the time. Often, our salvation comes from the unlikeliest of people and connections. I drive across town to North Texas State University and move into the dorm. As planned, I tape my Cheap Trick and Led Zeppelin posters on my side of the room, prep my shower caddy with shampoo and soap.

And then I descend into hell.

Every day, I'm breaking inside. I watch the girls preening for the boys. Watch them wanding mascara through the perfect eyelashes of their perfect eyes, and I would give anything to be one of them. I'm not pretty anymore. I will never be pretty. Never be "normal." I'm disfigured. A freak. And my freakish appearance makes most people uncomfortable, as if, simply by being in my presence, they might catch the bad luck of me. Looking at me makes them feel guilty for having escaped one of fate's cruel turns in the road. People are not to be hated for this. A certain amount of denial is necessary for getting through life. At its best, it allows us to ride the roller coaster, drive cars, fly in planes. At its worst, it ignores the human-ness of other humans. It denies that misfortune happens, and that sometimes people need help, not scorn or shame. "You have a great personality" has never felt so awful to hear. Fact: Freshman boys are not judging your personality first. I am mostly invisible. When I am visible, it's worse. A girl on my floor sees my driver's license with the "before" picture of me. "What happened to you?" she asks with obvious distaste, as if my face were a messy table in a restaurant that needs cleaning before she'll even think of sitting down. And then, with a shake of her head, "You were so pretty."

One day on campus, I run into a man who used to frequent

the independent bookstore where I worked the summer before my senior year of high school. He doesn't recognize me, and I have to tell him who I am. "I was in an accident," I say, the words a reflex now. "Oh, I wondered," he says, after I give him the CliffsNotes version. "I mean, one side of your face is still beautiful, but the other side looks like Frankenstein."

Every night I go to bed with the same prayer: "Please, God, make this go away." And every morning, for those first few seconds before reality creeps in, I dream that I'm my old self and everything is as it was. But it's not. It's the new normal, which is not normal, but fucked up and frightening and alienating. I know that I'm mortal now. Eighteen-year-olds are not supposed to have a firm grasp on just how easily they can die. They're supposed to take risks. Each time I get into a car as either a passenger or driver is a full-on panic attack. I can't drive above forty miles an hour, can't even think about getting on the highway. With no depth perception, I can't judge how near or far the car in front of me is. And looking to my left to merge into oncoming traffic is a nightmare.

It becomes my routine to wait for my roommate to leave, then anesthetize myself by getting high—booze, pills, pot, speed, whatever's handy—and listen to side four of The Who's *Quadrophenia*. It's the musical story of Jimmy, a working-class speed-freak mod in mid-1960s England, alienated from his family, desperate for more than the world offers, rejected by the girl he loves, and lost in his own fractured mind ("I'm not schizophrenic; I'm bleeding quadrophenic"). The music is beautiful and sharp with pain and longing. It's an exquisite sadness that makes me feel seen and understood. Sometimes, hope is an album written by an angry British rock star about an angry, alienated speed-freak boy who understands your pain. Sometimes, hope is a song or a book or TV show, anything that makes you feel connected to the rest of the world. Something that reminds you that you are not alone in your pain.

"Is it me for a moment?" the song asks. "The stars are falling. The heat is rising. The past is calling."

Like the stars in the song, I am falling. It's getting harder and harder for me to attend classes. Get out of bed. Change clothes. Take a shower. EJ stops by one day after her last class and tries to pull me from the bed. "You have to get up!" Her blond perfection is an affront. She is my best friend, and I resent her for her beauty, for the boys who follow her around like eager puppies. It's unfair, of course. She's had plenty of bad breaks and will go on to have many more. But that's what the absence of hope does in the throes of a deep depression: It works like a Pro Tools vocal compressor, squeezing all the highs and lows into a flat tonality. I am alone. More fundamentally alone than I have ever been in my life. Like an astronaut whose line has come untethered in space, I float into a vast, silent dark.

On the worst of these nights, I go to a party with EJ and a few other girls from my dorm. While they primp and prep excitedly, I keep trying to put eyeliner on my left eye. The prosthesis waters constantly, washing away my work until I give up. I don't want to go to this party. I'm so raw around the edges, it's as if my messy pain is on the outside, falling around me in sickening glops as I walk; the brave-not-sad act is wearing out. EJ alters the dates on our driver's licenses with an X-Acto knife so we appear to be above the drinking age. As she performs surgery on my ID, it feels symbolic somehow. I'm no longer the girl in that DMV photo. I feel older. Older than I should. My roommate, who is dating my brother, has gone to Waco for the weekend with him. She's left behind her purse, which has a slot in front with a plastic covering for an ID. It will further obscure the X-Acto knife work. *Perfect*, I think, slinging the purse over my shoulder.

At the party, my cute friends are surrounded by flirtatious boys. But no boy will talk to me for longer than is politely necessary. It's as if my damaged face has rendered me invisible. I stand on the outside of the circle. As it turns out, my roommate has forgotten her birth control pills in the purse I've borrowed. After an hour of searching, she finally tracks me down at the party, furious. "I'm sorry. I thought you were gone," I say over and over. The commotion is embarrassing me. I don't want to draw attention. Don't want people looking at me. At my face. She flounces off toward my brother's waiting car, purse in tow. He rises from the driver's side and yells across the front lawn: "You stupid fucking . . ." Well, let's just say it's a word that rhymes with punt. Then they peel out, leaving me there on the lawn. Everyone turns to look now. Everyone turns to look at the freak who is also a stupid effing rhymes-with-punt. Someone nearby laughs, "Oh my God." My humiliation is complete. When everyone turns back to their keg-pumping and mating rituals, I leave the party. No one notices. *Don't cry, don't cry, don't cry,* I tell myself with each slap of my sandals on the sidewalk. As I climb the stairs to my floor, I consider taking all the painkillers I've got left—ten, fifteen pills—and checking out for good. Why not? What's left? This will be my life forever. This pain will never end.

The thought of that future squeezes the air from my lungs. Alone in my dorm room, I put on side four of *Quadrophenia*. I grip the pill bottle in one hand. And then I sob as if something has come loose inside me. As if I am so broken, there will never be any putting me back together.

As if there is no chance of hope ever again.

The beautiful thing about hope is that it doesn't give up on you. It waits around for you to notice it. Like being up early enough to catch the sunrise. Seeing that first pink light fall across a dewy spiderweb. Realizing how much beauty and life continues while you're feeling lost. For just a moment, you're found. A moment may be all you need to continue to the next moment. Hope is patient. And stronger than you can imagine. Emily Dickinson said that "Hope is the thing with feathers." You ever looked at a feather? Everybody always thinks about the soft, velvety floss. But a feather's got a fucking spine inside it. That spine is flexible enough for flight; it's tough enough to hold all that floss together. Put enough feathers together and you've got wings to carry you forward. Fucking hope, man. It's good stuff.

That night, all I know is that I need to get the pain inside me out somehow. I don't care how. That's when I pick up the little yellow journal still packed in my milk crate of stuff. I crack it open. Blank pages stare back at me. Where to start? How to say what must be said? I make my first entry on the second page: "I don't know why I didn't write on the first page. I hate to devirginize anything, I guess."

One sentence. Then another. And just like that, it's begun. I'm writing myself back into existence. "Is it me for a moment?" *Quadrophenia* asks. It is. The new me. The one emerging. The one who will keep writing, first to stay alive, then because it's all I want to do. Because there is so much life to write about. I write as a willful act of reconstruction. I am building a self with each word, each phrase, each sentence. When I close the journal, I am exhausted. But I am also still alive.

I crawl into bed. For the first time in weeks, I sleep well.

It would be tempting to end here on this little fist pump of airbrushed hope that the magazine stories and feel-good ad campaigns really love. But that's bullshit, and I always vowed I'd never bullshit you. The truth is, hope is a bit like a muscle you have to exercise, and mine needed plenty of help. Hope is sometimes less a freeze-frame-worthy "Hell yeah!" than it is a series of adjustments you make over time, a different way of seeing. Of being in the world. And so I think it's important to tell you that I spent many more months trying and failing, punishing myself and feeling lost in pain.

I think it's important to tell you two more quick stories.

At the end of that terrible year, on a night when hope bangs on the window trying to get my attention but I ignore it, I go to a party where I feel as if my soul is imploding and all my effort goes toward holding my smile in place. *Look at me! I'm not sad! I am the life of the party!* Along the way, I get very fucked up. Somewhere around Too-Far-Gone O'Clock, I climb up onto the bar to prove that I *absolutely-positively-can-so-tap-dance-just-watch-this-y'all*. The minute I stand up, I am whacked in the head by a whirring ceiling fan. The metal blades slash through my forehead fast as Ginsu knives. I tumble to the floor, laughing as, once again, blood courses over my face and down my shirt. In the emergency room, the seen-it-all doctor on call informs me, once again, that there's good news and bad news. Bad news: I need twenty-five stitches to close the wounds in my head, and since I'm higher than a kite, he can't give me any pain medication. The good news? I probably won't feel it in my state. He's right on both counts—it takes exactly twenty-five stitches and I don't feel a thing.

In the sober light of early morning, I sure do. My skull pounds as I make my way to my mother's house. I am lost, lost, so lost. She opens the door, takes one look at my gauze-wrapped head seeping blood and the shirt that looks as if I've been to an all-night massacre, and puts a hand to her mouth.

"Please don't say anything," I beg. I'm starting to cry now, the whole ugly year rising up inside me like a wounded animal howling in the wilderness, desperate for some small comfort. It takes a long time for the words to form in my gut and fight their way up my throat and onto my tongue. "You have to help me get out of here or I'm going to die. And I am so tired of dying."

Sometimes hope is asking for help because you need someone else's hope to light the way. Everyone needs help now and then. There is no shame in it, my loves. My mother calls my father. They make more calls. It seems they've been wanting to help but had no idea how to reach me out in space. Within weeks, I'm enrolled at the University of Texas at Austin. I am starting over. Starting fresh.

In August, I move into another dorm in Austin, where I still do not feel completely at home yet. Where I still believe myself weird and ugly and unworthy and all of those lies. But I'm working on it. I've packed new hope for this trip. The sort of hope borne of a year of grit and hurt, of being shattered and slowly rebuilt, inside and out. I'm growing a feather's spine. I meet others like me: misfits and weirdos and freaks. People who come trailing suitcases of pain but also dreams. Soon enough, I find I do belong. We begin making a world of our own. There are sing-alongs on rooftops and epic dinner parties and performances with a comedy troupe where no one tells me I need two eyes to be onstage. I've brought the yellow journal. Through it all, I keep writing, braiding myself a lifeline with words.

More and more, hope is a pen.

Last month, I cleaned out my desk. Its drawers were chock-full of Things I Could Not Live Without—my son's artwork from elementary school, a parody gossip rag EJ and I wrote in middle school, letters from my college friend Laurie the year she moved to Hollywood and her life was dusted with odd magic and sometimes just the odd, love notes from my husband, birth certificates and death certificates and my grandmother's diary from 1927 in which she wrote, on the anniversary of her fifteen-year-old brother's death, "Today is a hard day." Sometimes, there are hard days. Days stretched so tight with pain that they seem as if they can allow no room for hope.

But it's there. I promise you, it is there.

Despite the many surgeries to try to "fix" me, I still have a wonky eye, a misshapen nose, and a lopsided smile. And these days, lines crinkle the corners of my eyes and mouth, a legacy from decades of laughter, late nights with friends, worry over a sick child, running on beaches under bright sun. My face is a map of all I have lived. Some days, I feel beautiful and right in my skin. Some days, I don't. The truth is, we never really get fixed; instead, we try to make peace, daily, with who and what we are. We learn to embrace the glorious, imperfect whole rather than punishing ourselves because of our flawed parts.

Anyway.

Wedged behind a stack of envelopes was the little yellow journal from my freshman year. For decades, I hadn't been able to open it. This time, I sat and read, turning its musty pages, marveling at that girl fighting to survive the pain threatening to take her under. I felt such love and compassion for her. And I knew how hopeful her future would be. I knew that girl would make New York City her home. She would find true love and marriage, joyous motherhood, and many wonderful friends. She would stay friends with EJ forever, the two of them laughing so hard at times, they'd fall on the floor, gasping for breath. She would travel far, wandering the tiny alleyways of Venice, blowing kisses to the moon above the *ramblas* of Barcelona, drinking coffee from delicate cups in a Vienna café. She would take with her resilience, compassion for other hurting people, and deep reserves of strength. The sort of strength with roots. The strength that comes from vulnerability, from giving up on the pursuit of perfection, which is a punishing way to live, and embracing all the messiness instead. She would find hope's best friend, forgiveness—for her own failings and for the failings of others. We're all works in progress, after all, and forgiveness is really the only way forward. And she would write. Her life would be filled with glorious words. Words to make sense of herself and the world. Words to bridge the distance between what is felt deep in the soul and what seems impossible to say. Words that connect. Words that heal. Such wonder to come. So much to feel hopeful about.

What I'm saying, my loves, is this: You may not recognize hope when it comes to you. It doesn't always come holding a giant hope banner, waving streamers and playing kazoos, leading a parade of better days. Sometimes, it whispers gently to you from a ratty old chair in a corner at the far edge of sunlight breaking through the gloom: "Hey. It's okay. I'm here." It comes as a feeling in your gut that the person judging you only by your looks isn't worth your precious time. It might even come disguised as a little yellow journal and a pen and a desk under the glow of a bare bulb when you feel marooned in your loneliness and despair, thinking yourself ugly and unlovable and worthless, certain that no good thing will ever stop into the roadside diner of your soul ever again. Once you recognize hope in all of its disguises, it becomes easier to spot. There. There it is. Right there. Do you see it? It's standing beside you. It is within you. It's all around, ready when you are, patient, so patient.

You are not alone.

You are not alone.

You are not alone.

HOPE NATION

DAVID LEVITHAN   LIBBA BRAY   **ANGIE THOMAS**

ALLY CONDIE   MARIE LU   JEFF ZENTNER

NICOLA YOON   KATE HART   GAYLE FORMAN

CHRISTINA DIAZ GONZALEZ   ATIA ABAWI

ALEX LONDON   HOWARD BRYANT   ALLY CARTER

ROMINA GARBER   RENÉE AHDIEH   AISHA SAEED

JENNY TORRES SANCHEZ   NIC STONE

JULIE MURPHY   I. W. GREGORIO   JAMES DASHNER

JASON REYNOLDS   BRENDAN KIELY

ANGIE THOMAS

Now More Than Ever

FACT: FOR MANY OF US, our current political climate is scary.

Fact: It's okay to be afraid, overwhelmed, and stressed.

Fact: I've got more hope now than I had before November 8, 2016.

As a young black woman living in Mississippi, I've unfortunately felt the frustration, pain, anger, and stress that many people in this country are just starting to feel because of our current political climate. My home state is known more for its bigotry than for anything else. Now, let me set the record straight: I've never been told to sit at the back of the bus. I've never had to drink from a "blacks only" water fountain. I've never even seen a KKK member in my life. Mississippi is still problematic in many ways, but it is not *that* problematic. The bigotry comes in a different form now.

For one, there's our state flag, straight from the Confederacy. Many of the state's white citizens cannot seem to understand how a flag associated with a racist past offends the state's black citizens. (Fact: Way too many Mississippians have trouble letting go of the past and embracing a more inclusive future.) Then there are the elected officials who make comments on social media about "lynching" flag opponents. On top of that, there are the laws that are clearly rooted in bigotry, like the so-called "religious freedom" law, which is really just a way to allow people to legally discriminate against the LGBTQIA+ community. (As a Christian, I wish more Mississippians would remember that Jesus said to love our neighbors. There's no "except if they . . ." at the end of that.) I can't forget the attempts to make sagging pants illegal. A law like that would clearly target young black men above all. (I seriously doubt plumbers would get into trouble.)

Yep, Mississippi is problematic. Yep, our country currently is too. Yep, I still have hope.

Like so many, I had a moment of despair on Election Night. Everything that I hoped wasn't true about our country and the people in it suddenly seemed to be. Months before the election, I was trolled big-time by hate groups on Twitter simply because I asked people to stand up for diversity. On Election Night, it felt as if those individuals had won, and I almost wondered why we should even try to change things.

Then my book came out.

The Hate U Give may be one of the scariest things I will ever publish. I put a lot of my own emotions into that book, and sharing those feelings with the world is scary. Even more than that, I was terrified of what the reception to the book would be. It's inspired by the Black Lives Matter movement, and if you say "Black Lives Matter" to three different people, you're likely to get thirty different responses. For some people like me, those words are a rallying cry, asking for a system that places value on black lives. For some, it dismisses the value of all other lives, and they say things like "All Lives Matter" or "Blue Lives Matter." For others, the movement and the organization are hateful or antiwhite. I hoped that my book would help people truly understand why we say "Black Lives Matter," and why we feel as if we have to constantly remind this country of the value of our lives. Yes, all lives should indeed matter, but we have a systemic problem in this country in which black lives don't matter enough. So black lives matter too.

But after being trolled and seeing just how hateful people can be, I was hesitant for my book to even come out. I remember cautiously checking my email in the days and weeks after it was released, just waiting for the moment some bigot decided to send me hate mail. I wondered if I would have hecklers at events, like some authors of color have dealt with when they dare write about anything that confronts the racism of this country. And my launch event in Mississippi? Mississippi, where racism still rears its ugly head? I had no idea what might happen, especially when the event was advertised on the local news as a launch party for the "Black Lives Matter–inspired novel."

Yet over the past few months, the love I've received from *The Hate U Give* has stunned me. There are three encounters in particular that will most likely stay with me.

As I said, my launch party was held in Mississippi. It was in my hometown of Jackson, to be exact. As the capital city, Jackson has a tainted history. If you know anything about the civil rights movement, you will know that many sit-ins and marches took place there. A civil rights leader by the name of Medgar Evers was murdered in 1963 in his driveway while his young children were inside the home— my family's house is only minutes away from his. In fact, my mom was a kid at the time and heard the gunshots that killed him.

Like the rest of the state, Jackson cannot seem to get away from its past and is still divided in many ways. There's the mostly black side of Jackson and the mostly white side of Jackson. These racial lines seem to be economic lines as well. The mostly black parts of Jackson are the run-down parts where you don't go unless you absolutely have to and the schools perform poorly. In other words, they are mostly the hood. It's the total opposite with the mostly white areas. And racism? It's a hot topic that people either don't want to discuss or will passionately discuss, but it's obviously still a factor in many ways.

So, my launch party. I remember sitting at my signing table and looking out at the line of people, stretched out the door, who were there to meet me. I will be honest—one of the first things I noticed was how many white individuals were in line. Yes, right there in Jackson, Mississippi, half of the hundreds of people waiting to see me and get me to sign my Black Lives Matter book were white. It was a moment that caused me to check my own biases. I remember one gentleman in particular. He was older, white, and not exactly who I had in mind as I wrote my book, but he thanked me for it. He hadn't read a word of it yet, but he said he already knew it was an important story, even for an "old guy like me who's still trying to get it right."

I never thought someone would say that to me, and especially not in Mississippi.

Only days after my launch party, I did an East Coast tour to promote my book. There were so many great memories made along the way as I was blessed to connect with readers and soon-to-be readers. One of the highlights was my event in Maplewood, New

Jersey. Just across the river from NYC, it's a very picturesque small township that looks like it came straight off a postcard. However, even with Maplewood as diverse as it is, the town had recently experienced racist incidents at the local high school. It was a story that was being repeated in many schools around the country after the election as hate crimes seemed to increase—racist graffiti had been tagged on bathroom walls, and racial slurs were being thrown around by students. By the time I arrived to the town for my event, the incidents had made the national news. I didn't know what to expect.

My event was almost like a town hall meeting. The mayor introduced me along with the moderator, a professor from Harvard. The venue was packed. Hundreds of people of all races and ethnicities showed up just to hear me discuss my book. They actually cared about what I, the black girl from the hood in Mississippi, had to say about Black Lives Matter.

Toward the end, we held a question-and-answer session. One of the first people to get up was a black woman who had lived in the town most of her life. She talked about how the recent incidents at the school hurt her and asked not just me but everyone there at the event two important questions: Can we begin to listen to one another, and can we change things?

The questions got a lot of applause. Some people answered and told her that's exactly why they were at my event—they wanted to help change things. Instead of ignoring race issues brought up by people of color, more and more of them were determined to listen. That's honestly one of the most important steps to change, especially in our current political climate. It's easy to write people off when it comes to racism, bigotry, and hatred. Instead, we need to pay attention to the concerns people raise. If I say that something is racist, it doesn't help for you to tell me I'm just making it up or exaggerating. Listen. Learn. Grow.

The folks in Maplewood are trying to do just that. Imagine if more cities and towns did the same thing.

It gives me hope.

By the time my tour was over, I'd heard many stories and witnessed many things that gave me some light in the darkness. However, it was an email that seemed to top even all of those incidents.

Like I said earlier, I used to dread checking my email. I just knew that at some point, a bigot would get ahold of my address and send me hate mail or threats because of my book. One day, I received an email with the subject line "Thank you." Simple, yet I was cautious. Subject lines can be deceptive on purpose. I opened the email. The writer started it by telling me she had been raised by a white supremacist. Honestly, I tensed up, waiting for the vitriol.

Instead, she poured her heart out to me.

She told me about her father and some of the things he had said and done over the years, and how it shaped her view of the world and black people in particular. The n-word was a regular part of his vocabulary, among other things. As she got older, she started to second-guess the things he'd told her and began to realize they were rooted in hatred—and she wanted to change. Books allowed her to do that. Professor Rudine Sims Bishop once described books as being mirrors, windows, and sliding glass doors. For this woman who wrote me, books gave her a window that helped her humanize people she was once taught were beneath her. How powerful is that?

Recently, someone had told her to read my book. According to her, it opened her eyes even more. She now understood a little more why we say Black Lives Matter. Even more than that, she had a better understanding that black lives do indeed matter. By stepping into Starr's shoes for four-hundred-plus pages, she gained insight. More importantly, she developed empathy. It made her look at the Starrs and the Khalils of the world in a whole different light.

I'm honored to know that my words did that.

Since November 8, 2016, we have witnessed a horrendous side of our country. More of us have come to realize that in many ways, the past is still present—racism and bigotry didn't die, they just hid themselves well. Now it seems they no longer have reasons to hide.

However, for me, the days after November 8 have shown me that there is more love in this country than I thought, there are more reasons to keep going, and there are more people who are trying to change things than I realized. Now more than ever, people are speaking out and getting involved. My book has allowed me to see this through one-on-one conversations with people, and I hope you see it through the rallying cries echoing around this country. We are not being silent, we are not sitting down, we are not allowing hatred to win.

We are fighting for you, and we will continue to fight.

You give me hope. I hope I give you hope too.

DAVID LEVITHAN   LIBBA BRAY   ANGIE THOMAS

ALLY CONDIE   MARIE LU   JEFF ZENTNER

NICOLA YOON   KATE HART   GAYLE FORMAN

CHRISTINA DIAZ GONZALEZ   ATIA ABAWI

ALEX LONDON   HOWARD BRYANT   ALLY CARTER

ROMINA GARBER   RENÉE AHDIEH   AISHA SAEED

JENNY TORRES SANCHEZ   NIC STONE

JULIE MURPHY   I. W. GREGORIO   JAMES DASHNER

JASON REYNOLDS   BRENDAN KIELY

ALLY CONDIE

Rundown

I HAVE TWO RECURRING DREAMS. I've had them since high school. The first dream is one a lot of people have. It's the one where you want to run but your legs won't move.

My *I can't run* dream is very specific. It's always a certain place and under a certain circumstance. In my dream, I'm not running *away* from anything. I'm trying to get to a finish line. A very specific finish line. The finish line of the Cedar City High School cross-country course. I know every inch of that course the way you only know terrain you have covered in pain.

I know the hillocks in the grass up on the long stretch between the baseball fields and the Walmart, the part where no one ever walks up to cheer because it's boring and far away. I hear the whisk of the grass against my shoes, my own breathing, my heart thudding, and the sounds of runners behind me.

I know the *click click click* sound of my racing shoes on the sidewalk as I bear down on the curve near the seminary building, ready to take the short steep hill right by the school and the parking lot.

I could run that course in my sleep, and I do.

It always happens near the end. Where I've covered all the hard,

hard ground of the course and I'm in the little hollow of grass just before the track, and all I have to do is run half a lap of the track and I'll be at the finish line.

So close.

But in my dream, in that hollow of grass so near the finish, I go down. My legs stop working, and I fall to the ground, grass-staining my knees and looking up to see the feet of other runners, the soles of their shoes flashing past me like the underbellies of fish at the bottom of the ocean.

And I can't get back up.

When I'm twelve years old, my grandfather dies.

My grandfather and I are close, but not so close that I understand he is dying until he is dead. I didn't know he wasn't going to come back from the hospital. Before the hospital, he met me every day after school with Hostess cupcakes, pretending he had baked them himself. I knew he was joking, and I played along. He had the best, deepest voice in the world. A grandfather-clock voice. Every month, we'd go on a date and he held the door for me. He never let me pay, even though I gave him the date-a-month gift as his Christmas present. One time we got ice cream. Another time we went to the café on Main Street for hot chocolate and cinnamon toast. Even though I'm shy around adults, I never worry about what I'm going to say to my grandfather or what we'll talk about. He is comfortable and beloved. He always wears an ironed white shirt, dark-framed glasses, and shiny shoes. He smells like mints.

I cry all the way through the funeral service, and my aunt has to pass tissues down the row to me. I knew I would cry, but I didn't understand until this moment how it feels to be unable to stop. My father plays a song on the piano during the service—"Wishing You Were Somehow Here Again" from *Phantom of the Opera*. When my grandmother has to follow the casket out, she stumbles a little, but she catches herself quickly. I love her so much it hurts.

"How do you think he got to heaven?" one cousin asks another at the graveside service.

Some of my family is religious, and they're positive that my grandfather is in heaven. My parents are not religious, and they have no doubt he's there in the ground.

"We'll see him again someday," says one aunt.

"We'll never see him again," say my parents.

Some of us cousins aren't sure who is right.

But my little cousin Caitlin has answers. Caitlin is three and a half, and she has bangs and freckles. She's so cute that whenever she comes to visit, I pretend she's my little sister. "*I* know," Caitlin says. "There's a red button in his coffin, and he pushed it and it sent him to heaven."

She's so certain that we all pause to think about this, even the older cousins like me who should know better.

"That's dumb," says a cousin. "He was dead. He couldn't have pushed a button."

"Well then," says Caitlin, "somebody pushed it *for* him."

She leaves us standing at the grave and walks off with perfect assurance.

• • •

A few weeks after my grandfather dies, my mother has to go to the hospital and stay there for a long time.

This is because she's pregnant with twins. Two baby girls. But one of them has died. Everything was going fine until it wasn't. One morning, my mom woke up and knew that something was wrong.

The other twin is alive, but it's a waiting game. They need to keep my mom pregnant long enough that the living twin has a chance to survive, but not so long that the dead twin makes the environment in the womb so toxic that it kills the living twin.

This is something I can't think about too much, and my mom says she is the same way. She's very patient in the hospital where we go to visit her. The walls are pink. She has a TV to watch, and magazines and books by the side of the bed to read, and lots of people who love her come and visit her. Even so, I can't imagine a stranger place for my mom to be.

My mother likes to hike and do yoga and create art, and she is *never* still. Before the hospital, she couldn't even watch a television show all the way through. Or a basketball game. Not even the Jazz, whom she likes a lot when they are in the playoffs. She'd peek in to see how things were going and then off she'd go again, to water the flowers outside or grade papers or clean a bathroom.

But right now she's very still. She has to stay in bed, at the hospital, all day every day, except for when they let her get up to go to the bathroom. That's it.

"I never thought I'd look forward to going to the bathroom so much," my mom says when I visit her at the hospital, and we both laugh.

She is still great at laughing, and being beautiful.

I wish I knew that secret, to being beautiful. My mother is lovely.

She has wide brown eyes and a slender frame and a smile that lights up the room. I finally traded my glasses for contacts and my hair is not as bad as it has been, but I'm still awkward. I never have quite the right clothes. All the popular girls at my school are cowgirls, and my family doesn't even own a chicken. So I can't wear cowboy boots and stuff like that, because then I'd be a wannabe cowgirl, which is much worse than being nothing at all.

My dad's doing his best taking care of us kids, but he broke his wrist, which could have happened at a better time.

Things are not going great. Without my grandma, who makes us food and takes care of us during the day, we would be in trouble.

But I have a secret weapon.

A new best friend. He is the miracle of my seventh-grade year, and his name is Justin.

Justin and I understand each other even though we are not the same. Here are all the things that are different about us:

He is really, *really* Republican. Like, wants-to-be-the-president-someday Republican. He talks about it all the time. He knows more about politics than most adults I know, let alone any of the other seventh graders.

I am a Democrat. I think. I know it's what my parents are. I know I care like crazy about everyone having a chance and also the environment.

Justin knows what it's like to be popular.

I don't.

His family belongs to the main religion in Utah.

Mine doesn't.

Here is what we have in common:

When we met each other, we clicked. It started because we would laugh at the same things that no one else was laughing at, and we started to catch each other's eye across the room when that happened. We're both smart and get good grades.

We both have good families and friends but are often lonely on the inside.

We both have dark hair and very alert eyebrows.

I'm not supposed to talk on the phone with Justin. My parents have a lot of rules in general, and a lot of rules about boys and talking to them and hanging out with them.

But. My mom is in the hospital and my dad is really busy.

So I sneak and call him. I stretch the phone into the linen closet and pray that it will be his nice mom who answers when I call and not his intimidating, football-playing high school brothers.

Justin doesn't always say the right thing. In fact, this is another thing we have in common. A lot of the time he says the *wrong* thing, which happens to me too. For example, everyone teases us about dating, and we're only friends. But no one will believe it. We *want* people to believe it, because we both have crushes on other people, so we decide to tell everyone that we're cousins and that's why we spend all our time together.

That turns out to be the wrong thing to say.

Everyone ends up thinking that we're cousins who are dating, which is disgusting and embarrassing.

But here is the thing about Justin.

He is there.

And he makes me laugh all through the months my mom is in the hospital.

I swear I have an endorphin rush every time I talk to him because he's just. so. funny. And he feels the same way about me. I have never made anyone laugh the way I make Justin laugh.

With the help of my secret weapon, I am okay even though two people whom I love have died.

Someone so old.

Someone so new, who never even got a chance to start.

My dad wakes me up one morning. "Your grandma's on her way over," he says. "I'm going to be with your mom. She's having the baby."

It's time.

Can it be time?

Is it too soon?

Too late?

My little sister is born. She weighs four pounds, seven ounces and is seven weeks early. She can breathe without help, but can't eat on her own yet, and she'll have to stay in the NICU until she's five pounds.

She made it.

I can't wait to tell Justin at school. I find him in the hallway near Mrs. Fotheringham's class, which we have together. "My sister's here," I say. "My parents named her Hope."

When we go to see her, Hope looks like she has been through the wringer. She is tiny and her legs and arms are dangly, and she has a tube in her nose. She opens her eyes, and they are weary and dark and huge.

Several years later, in high school, I have depression.

It appears to be triggered by a physical event—a bout with

severe anemia. "Yours is so bad that a few years ago we would have hospitalized you for blood transfusions," says my doctor, "but now we'll give you shots."

The shots are iron shots right in your hip, ones that leave enormous bruises for weeks. But I'm relieved there is a solution. I have been exhausted, my cross-country race times getting slower even though I've been working harder. My legs feel like lead, and I can't move the way I want.

This is when I begin to have the running dream, the one where I can't finish the race.

When we find out about the anemia, I'm almost happy. Now we know why I feel so bad. In a matter of a few weeks, the shots have done the trick. My hematocrit levels are back in normal range. There is oxygen moving through my bloodstream again, and my legs are lighter. At the state meet I have the race of my life. I make the All-State team, and we win the overall championship as a team. We hold the trophy over our heads, and our coach is so proud, he cries.

So why don't I feel better in my mind?

Why do I keep having the dream where I can't run?

And there's another dream now. I'm in my grandparents' house, the place I love best on earth. It's after school and I come inside, just like I do every day. I walk through the swinging doors in the hallway, notice myself in the pictures push-pinned into the bulletin board in the hall. No one is in the kitchen. "Hello!" I call out, sure of my place in this house, sure in knowing that here I am loved and cherished by both my grandparents. I hear a creak in the master bedroom, directly above the kitchen, which means my grandfather has heard my call. He suffers from vertigo and has to lie down during the day, but if he knows I'm in the house, he *always* comes downstairs to see me. *Creak.*

In my mind, I can see him rising from the bed where he's been resting on top of the covers. I can picture him putting on his glasses, smoothing down the front of his white button-up shirt.

But then he doesn't come down.

Because he is dead.

I remember this before I wake up. That's how the dream ends, with the realization that he's gone. It hurts every time.

It kind of feels like everything hurts inside.

"I think you need some help," my mom tells me. She says it kindly, and without shaming. "I felt really down and sad after Hope was born. Like you feel now."

Yeah, but you had a reason, I think. You had lost a baby. You were taking care of a newborn. You were sleep deprived and had gone through something huge. I haven't gone through anything like that. A small health crisis, now solved. A breakup with a boyfriend I really liked.

We find a therapist and my doctor recommends medication. It takes a while for it all to work.

When I am in the worst of my depression, when I can't even pretend I care and all I'm really doing is sitting on the porch swing in front of my house and looking out at the mountains and the lights, Justin sits next to me and cries. "I don't know what to do to help you," he says.

I don't cry. I don't really even talk to him. I don't call him anymore, but he calls me and comes over, sometimes fresh from his job as a janitor at the hospital. He's wearing scrubs and looks very tired.

As the summer and fall go on, I do feel better. I go on all-day hikes with my friends, including Justin. We have to wade through water with canyons rising on both sides, and pack in our lunches and scramble over rocks. We leave early in the morning and come home late at night, sunburned, with sand in our shoes. We decide to train for a marathon, and we go on long runs in the morning together, on roads where the only people we see are farmers in their pickup trucks. They lift one hand from the steering wheel to wave at us. We start early in the morning, when it's cool in the high desert, and by the last miles the sun has always hunted us down. We're careful when we run over the cattle guards in the road so we don't twist our ankles. At the beginning, we usually talk, but by the end we're too tired. It feels good, though, to be tired in this way. When we run the marathon in October, it's not easy for either Justin or me, but we both finish. I wish I could tell my grandfather. He would have been so proud, and probably surprised. No one else in my family is a runner, and I didn't start until a year or two after he died.

There's no red button to eject you straight into heaven. No button to shoot you past depression and into happiness.

But.

There are these things.

A friend who will sit with you.

An adult who will have experienced their own mental illness and who will not think it is embarrassing to talk about it or to get help.

A little sister named Hope who loves you and thinks you're the best even when you are quite sure you are *not*. She'll tell you this joke she made up, over and over: "What if there were a cow . . . *on your head?*" and she will think it's funny every single time.

You may not have all of these things.

You may have different ones.

But.

Also.

You might have this.

As you grow older, and even if you still have the dreams (I do), you'll know that hope can be born even when things have gone and you can't have them back.

Someone will say something, ask for help, and your heart will know a part of what they're experiencing. Not exactly what they are going through—no one can ever know that—but enough.

You'll know to stay on the swing.

And listen.

DAVID LEVITHAN LIBBA BRAY ANGIE THOMAS
ALLY CONDIE **MARIE LU** JEFF ZENTNER
NICOLA YOON KATE HART GAYLE FORMAN
CHRISTINA DIAZ GONZALEZ ATIA ABAWI
ALEX LONDON HOWARD BRYANT ALLY CARTER
ROMINA GARBER RENÉE AHDIEH AISHA SAEED
JENNY TORRES SANCHEZ NIC STONE
JULIE MURPHY I. W. GREGORIO JAMES DASHNER
JASON REYNOLDS BRENDAN KIELY

MARIE LU

Surviving

I WAS FIVE YEARS OLD in 1989, the year I left for America and the year the Chinese government cracked down on college-age protesters in Beijing's Tiananmen Square.

I was a kid. So, my memories of that time are simple and fragmented. The protests had been happening all throughout the spring of that year, culminating in a hundred thousand people filling the square, each calling for democracy. At the time, I lived near the square with my family—and for us, the sight of the weekly crowds was something of a tourist attraction. "Let's go see what the students are up to," my aunt would say, and she would wheel out her bicycle, help my cousin and me on, and then ride us out to the fringes of the square.

What *I* remember is keeping an eager eye out for the Popsicle vendors who set up shop around the square. I remember thinking that the sea of bicycles looked like a moving river. I remember the way my skin would stick to itself from the warm air.

And on the day the government finally cracked down, I remember the tanks out in the streets, waiting at the square's entrances for orders to come from above. I remember the massive, massive crowds, and my aunt leaning down to me, telling me that we should head home early. I remember that kindergarten was canceled the next day.

This kind of unrest was new and unusual to me, of course—I grew up in late-1980s China, a time of rapid economic growth and rising wealth. But my parents were all too familiar with events far worse; they had survived the Cultural Revolution, one of the darkest periods in China's history. To this day, my mother will not tell me all the things she witnessed during those dark days of her youth, but the stories she *has* shared sound like something out of a dystopian novel.

The way you survived during the revolution was to stay off the radar. My grandfather, an accomplished poet, burned every single one of his books. My mother's family flushed any family jewelry or valuables down the drain. They memorized Mao's "Little Red Book" in school while secretly studying on their own at home.

Whatever you did, your goal was to keep the Red Army's eyes from falling on you. Being *other* was dangerous.

I would listen to them tell these stories and think that some of them must be far too outlandish to be true. But then I would remember Tiananmen Square, and nod along.

It was that past world to which my parents said their goodbyes. It was that world my parents left behind, setting their sights instead on the light across the sea. And it was that world that cemented the fundamental lesson I thought we took with us to our new home:

Assimilation was the key to survival. You lived by keeping your head down. Do not rock the boat. Do not speak out. What was a better example of this than the Tiananmen Square Massacre? It's hard to say how many protesters died that day, but it was obvious to me that speaking up and standing out had killed them.

My father had already left for America—specifically, for Louisiana State University in Baton Rouge—a year earlier on a student visa that had taken ten years to acquire. Several months later, the travel visas for my mother and me were approved too, and we left to join him. He picked us up late at night in a beat-up yellow Cadillac that must have been on its last legs, and I rode back sandwiched in between my parents in the front seat, the ride so bumpy and the smell of old leather so pungent that I upchucked right onto my exhausted mother's shoes.

None of us spoke English yet, outside of the limited conversations my father could piece together. One of our first American experiences was Mardi Gras (of all things), and I can still remember us standing there on the street, feeling distinctly like an *other*, not understanding a word being said. What was this bizarre place where people dressed in costume and partied until morning? What was with all the shirtless people? Where were we? Why were we here?

We were incredibly poor. My parents rationed their food strictly—one orange a day, meat only on the weekends. Anything considered a treat was reserved for me, and eating out at fast-food restaurants was a luxury we almost never indulged in. On weekends, we searched for yard sale signs and church donation tents. Of course my parents couldn't afford child care, so my mother was forced to take me with her to her shifts at a local Chinese restaurant, where she learned to balance eight plates at once on her slim arms as I watched TV in the restaurant's broom closet from morning until evening, the only place anyone could keep a restless five-year-old.

I was as happy as a clam. Children adapt to almost anything when they're young, and my existence was the norm as far as I was concerned, because, well, what else could I compare it to? I was fed, clothed, sheltered, and loved. I took these privileges for granted and had absolutely no concept of poverty. In my protected little world, my hand-me-down stuffed toys were made of magic, and my summers in that broom closet were spent singing songs and making up my earliest stories to myself. We couldn't afford new clothes, but what did I care? My mother would spend weekends transforming reams of cheap cloth and unusable old shirts into the most beautiful dresses for me, full of lace and pockets and flower patterns. Our first Christmas, my father splurged on a tiny, two-foot-tall pine plant, and we excitedly decorated it with a single garland of lights and a dozen ornaments.

My parents were determined for us to adapt as quickly as possible, so we set about doing it in earnest. My mom gave me an assignment to go to kindergarten every day, write down five new English words I didn't know, memorize what they meant, and use them in sentences. I was encouraged not to speak Chinese at home. We watched American shows, cartoons, and movies. My parents put away our statue of the Guanyin Buddha, and every Sunday, I got on the little bus that took me to church, where I memorized Bible verses in exchange for plastic toy figurines.

I wrote English. I drew American cartoons. I played American video games. As my parents gradually found their footing—my father as an engineer, my mother as a software developer—and moved us to a more comfortable home in Texas, I adapted at an alarming speed. It wasn't long before my parents realized that, far from hoping I would be able to pick up English, they actually needed to worry about the fact that I no longer spoke Chinese at all. When I went to school, I wanted the brown paper bag lunch the other kids had—I wanted the Lunchables, the sandwich and juice, not the rice and fish my mom would pack for me. I was determined to shake off the *other* image, and I would accomplish that by erasing myself completely, by blending in with everyone else and following my adaptation rule: Stay quiet, be good.

It wasn't until I left for Los Angeles to attend the University of Southern California that I suddenly found myself immersed in an environment where everyone was an *other*—a bubble of young people thrust together into semi-independence for the first time in our lives.

I distinctly remember the sheer chaos on campus during my freshman year, and my surprise that all of these teenagers were *loud*—sometimes for trivial things, other times for global issues. The Iraq War had just begun, and there was a sense of electricity in the air, a campus-wide buzz of protest.

It baffled me at first. Look at these young people raising their voices, making decisions with real consequences! All I could think of was my memory of those college-age students gathered in Tiananmen Square, one hundred thousand of them, and the way the tanks had looked on.

Didn't my peers know the rule? Speaking out makes you a target, gets you killed. I stayed quiet.

One day, I walked past a table at which students were signing up to join a massive antiwar protest happening in San Francisco. I passed it on the first day, then the second and third day. On the fourth day, I stopped in front of the table to look at the sign-up sheet. I don't remember what compelled me to put my name down. But I did.

My mother, understandably, did not want me to go. I could hear the fear in her voice over the phone without even seeing her expression. It was dangerous, she told me, and I knew she was remembering her years in China, what she had seen and lived through. What could I say to justify my desire to go? It certainly wasn't bravery, or even a sense of justice and doing what was right. It was sheer curiosity, a reason my mother could never have afforded to use. What was a protest in America like? Would it resemble at all the only other protest I had ever witnessed, with tanks in the streets and soldiers facing off against civilians?

I went.

A sea of people. Deafening chants. Like the Tiananmen Square protests, there were a hundred thousand people protesting against the Iraq War. I remember standing on a bench with a half dozen of my classmates, holding a corner of our "USC Students Against the Iraq War" sign, and thinking about whether any of these students feared for their lives. Then I wondered if maybe those students in Tiananmen Square, those who were killed, would have demonstrated anyway, even if they had known what was going to happen to them.

The Iraq War protest was the first one I ever participated in. After it ended and I returned to school, I found myself sitting in on classes where I didn't belong, even if I got the occasional funny look. I signed up to join the student senate, even though I was incredibly awkward and anxious in public. I turned down law school and made a serendipitous decision to work on video games at Disney.

The version of me that had wanted to disappear would never have made these choices. They went against every lesson I'd ever learned about adaptation, about surviving via silence, about not rocking the boat.

But I realized that I had a fundamental misunderstanding of the lessons my parents had tried to teach me about adaptation. Never at any point in their journey did they survive by mere silence and assimilation. They did not make it out of the Cultural Revolution by keeping their heads down. When the world around them fell apart and their government refused to let them learn in school, they rebelled by studying secretly by candlelight at home. Instead of staying in China and falling into step, they left behind everyone they knew and loved and instead set out to a foreign, frequently hostile land. Somehow, somehow, they stood on their bedrock of disadvantage and built a foundation.

Being *other* was dangerous. And yet, my parents had—in defiance, optimism, and determination—still *chosen* to be other.

Survival was never about keeping your head down or not rocking the boat. It was about finding a way.

DAVID LEVITHAN   LIBBA BRAY   ANGIE THOMAS
ALLY CONDIE   MARIE LU   **JEFF ZENTNER**
NICOLA YOON   KATE HART   GAYLE FORMAN
CHRISTINA DIAZ GONZALEZ   ATIA ABAWI
ALEX LONDON   HOWARD BRYANT   ALLY CARTER
ROMINA GARBER   RENÉE AHDIEH   AISHA SAEED
JENNY TORRES SANCHEZ   NIC STONE
JULIE MURPHY   I. W. GREGORIO   JAMES DASHNER
JASON REYNOLDS   BRENDAN KIELY

JEFF ZENTNER

*Nobody Remembers the Names
of People Who Build Walls*

I SOMETIMES HEAR PEOPLE TALKING about how young people don't read anymore, and I think, *Are you kidding me?* Youth book culture has never been stronger. We're in a golden age of youth reading. And that's fortunate, because there is a simple truth, and if you've already figured this out, dear reader, and I'm sure you have, then that's great, but here it is:

Adults will let our youth down. Our highest institutions will let our youth down. What do I mean by that? I mean that people who lack empathy in their hearts will win important contests and be entrusted with great power, and they'll try to use that power to harm those who are weaker than them or different from them or whom our society has traditionally relegated to its margins. They'll try to use that power to limit the ability of those people they disfavor to lead joyful and complete lives, as full participants in our society. They'll use their positions of power to persuade frightened people to place the blame for their fears at the feet of people who have less power.

The world has always been thus, and to some extent, it will probably always be thus. I believe this stems from fundamental weaknesses in the human character, weaknesses that take a lot of work on the individual level to overcome. Work that many people aren't willing to do because it feels better to be selfish, because our society often elevates selfishness to a virtue. There have been times in our country's history when it's been easier to forget this, and I believe that you may be coming of age in a time when it is harder to forget this.

I believe there are tumultuous days ahead. You'll be entering adulthood during a time when many will be telling you that wrong is right, bad is good, and up is down.

Are you having fun so far? This is a fun essay, right? I'm more fun than a barrel of monkeys. Our world is dark and dangerous and full of evil. Good times! But I carry the flame of hope in my heart.

My hope lies in young Book People—probably you, if you're reading this. I believe one of the fundamental qualities needed to fight the gathering darkness of which I speak is empathy. Empathy is the ability to imagine yourself in someone else's shoes. To imagine what it would be like to be them. To feel their joy when they feel joyful. To feel their sorrow when they feel sorrowful. People of empathy do to others as they would have others do to them because they can imagine how terrible it would feel to be wronged.

And I believe that Book People are our brightest beacons of empathy. It takes great empathy to be so interested in the lives of other people that you don't even demand that they really exist. It takes great empathy to be able to so vividly imagine the lives and inner hearts of others that you can do it simply by reading ink symbols on slices of processed wood pulp.

In the days to come, you Book People will need to exercise your powers of empathy to help identify and fight those who would harm others. One of the best ways to do that is by standing with the people who are the targets of harm. The coming days will require that your empathy put on the armor of courage. They'll require you to love others more than you're afraid for yourself, because the only thing that drives out darkness is when love is more powerful than fear.

In the days to come, you need to allow your empathy to become an unstoppable force inside you, something that moves you to action. Something that won't let you stand idly by when evil happens in the world. It needs to become a force that makes you stand up with someone who's being abused in public. That makes you pick up the phone and make calls to lawmakers when you see something you know is wrong or harmful. That makes you lift your voice in support of people whose voices are unheard.

In the days to come, you Book People will have to be the keepers of our values. You will need to become the memory and the conscience of our nation. You will need to carry inside you a bright and inextinguishable flame.

Because we can't always count on the highest seats of power to remind us that the diversity of our nation is one of its greatest values. So it will fall to you. We can't always count on the highest seats of power to remind us that consent matters. So it will fall to you. We can't always count on the highest seats of power to honor facts and learning and wisdom. So it will fall to you. We can't always count on the highest seats of power to protect those in our society who have not been empowered to protect themselves. So it will fall to you. We can't always count on the highest seats of power to allow all Americans to live lives of joy, as full participants in society. So it will fall to you. We can't always count on the highest seats of power to stand for truth and correctness and honesty. So it will fall to you. We can't always count on the highest seats of power to stand against greed and corruption. So it will fall to you. We can't always count on the highest seats of power to stand for kindness and decency, so it will fall to you.

And all of this will require you to keep filling yourself with the best words and ideas, because these will be your sword and shield in the battles to come. It'll require you to keep filling yourself with the stories of courage and hope that make you feel strong and lift you up when you feel exhausted and hopeless. It'll require you to share these words and ideas with those who need them. It'll require you to create new stories filled with the best words and ideas. It'll require you to create new stories of courage and hope.

Nothing forces people to confront the humanity of others like engaging with their stories. Art softens hearts and teaches. It raises us up. Even those in the highest seats of power can be wounded and chastened by falling on the wrong side of art. So I hope, Book People, that you'll let the stories you love take root in you and grow and blossom and bear the fruit of other art. I hope that you'll tell your story so powerfully that no one can deny your humanity or anyone else's. I hope you'll tell stories so prescient and wise that no one can deny their lessons. I hope you'll tell stories so filled with hope that they set a fire in every heart that reads them. I hope you'll tell stories so filled with goodness that evil withers and turns to ash before them.

I know what it's like to have your life tip over into adulthood at a perilous and tumultuous time. On September 11, 2001, I was twenty-three years old, but still, I felt like a baby. I watched the towers of the World Trade Center burn, and I still remembered reading on the side of a packet of oatmeal that each tower had its own zip code. I must have been ten when I ate that oatmeal, but it still felt like yesterday. I got up on the morning of September 12, 2001, and went for a run, and the street was lined with American flags, and even though we were *united* against a common foe, I still felt the dread of knowing that I had inherited a world different from my parents' world. I felt the fear of sailing into uncharted waters.

During those dark days, I clung to stories, because stories are there for us in dark days. I know that days are coming that'll force me—that'll force all of us—to cling to stories for the strength to go on.

Sometimes I imagine how storytelling came about among the earliest humans, the ones older even than history. I imagine tiny, isolated bands of people crouched around fires, a tiny spot of warmth and light in a vast and cold darkness. They're surrounded by animals that are bigger than them. Faster. Stronger. With bigger teeth. Sharper claws. Thicker skin. Sharper eyesight. Better hearing. Keener noses. Faster reflexes.

But our ancestors had one very great advantage: a brain that could tell and understand stories. And so, one of them steps forward into the light and says, "Og want to tell story." (I feel like Og was a very popular name among cavemen.) And they say, "What's a story?" And Og says, "It good, it fun. Don't get too hung up on name. Og invent that." And then Og tells a story about them, in which they're brave and strong, and it looks like the saber-toothed tiger is going to beat them, but at the last second, they win. Oh, and by the way, there's some caveman romance (which I imagine involves a good deal of grunting). And the story makes them feel strong and brave, and maybe they sleep better that night, so when they go out to hunt the next day, they move a bit faster.

In difficult times, we can lean on stories as a source of strength and comfort. They can lift us and sustain us. I hope you'll seek out the stories that make you feel strong. I hope you'll share those stories so that other people can feel strong. I hope you'll create stories that make you feel strong and that make other people feel strong.

I can't pretend to fully know or understand what leads people to choose to make others feel alone and afraid. I don't know exactly why people love to seek and use power to prevent people different from them from living the most full and complete lives they can. I think it comes from a place of deep, unexamined fear of the unknown and the different. Maybe this fear used to serve a useful purpose in the survival of our species. Maybe our friend Og the Caveman was like, "Hey, what's that huge thing with black and orange stripes and walking on four legs instead of two? That's pretty different from me. I don't have orange and black fur! I better stay away from that thing!"

But if we indulge that instinct too far, we end up afraid of things and people we shouldn't be afraid of. The difference between you and a tiger is that the tiger wants to literally eat you. The difference between you and someone who loves people in a way that's different from you is that that person loves people in a way that's different from you. Here's where stories come in. They tell us the truth of other people's lives. They shine a light on shared humanity. They make us understand that we are different, but not *different*. That our differences are something that makes the human tapestry richer and more colorful, and not a threat.

You've heard of Anne Frank. You know her because you know her story. She wrote it down so that history couldn't deny her humanity. Who knows the name of the guy who invented the Berlin Wall? History does not honor the names of people who build walls. History does not honor the names of people who build monuments to fear and hatred. History honors the names of people who tear down walls. History honors the names of people who tell stories so powerful that walls crumble and fall before them. History honors the names of those who have the best ideas. Who walk the best paths. Who act with the most kindness and decency and empathy toward others. Who protect those who are being bullied and mistreated.

In the coming days, there's a question I want you to ask yourselves: "If not me, then who?" If not me, then who will stand for people whose voices aren't being heard? If not me, then who will stand for the right of all people to lead lives of joy and dignity? If not me, then who will stand for facts and reason and learning and truth? If not me, then who will stand for kindness? If not me, then who will stand for honesty? If not me, then who will stand for generosity? If not me, then who will stand for equality and justice?

I want you to demand that the people in power in our country uphold these values. I want alarm bells to go off in your head every time people in power talk about using the law to push around or punish people who are different from them—whether it's a difference in skin color, ethnicity, sexual orientation, religion, gender identity, ability, social class, or anything else that's being used to shove people into a corner. I want alarm bells to go off in your head because this is a failure of empathy. And without empathy, we have no society. We have a small group of powerful people and a lot of powerless people. Without empathy, we have a fundamentally and structurally unfair society in which some people enjoy incredible privilege and others enjoy none. I believe we can do better than that. I believe we *are* better than that.

I'm confident that your future is bright, Book People. I believe you'll laugh and fall in love and get married and lie on grass in the summertime and stare into the stars in wonder and build lives and hold your children and grandchildren, and read stories and write stories and create beauty and friendship, and lead lives of great joy. But more than any other generation that's come before you, you'll have to make it bright. Not just for yourselves, but for everyone.

I can't pretend to know everything that will happen in the days to come. But I know that stories are like fire. They give us light. They give us warmth. They burn things down so that new, green things can grow up and replace them.

Keep reading stories. Keep writing stories. Keep sharing stories. I will forever be at your side.

HOPE NATION

DAVID LEVITHAN   LIBBA BRAY   ANGIE THOMAS

ALLY CONDIE   MARIE LU   JEFF ZENTNER

NICOLA YOON   KATE HART   GAYLE FORMAN

CHRISTINA DIAZ GONZALEZ   ATIA ABAWI

ALEX LONDON   HOWARD BRYANT   ALLY CARTER

ROMINA GARBER   RENÉE AHDIEH   AISHA SAEED

JENNY TORRES SANCHEZ   NIC STONE

JULIE MURPHY   I. W. GREGORIO   JAMES DASHNER

JASON REYNOLDS   BRENDAN KIELY

NICOLA YOON

Love

MY HUSBAND SAYS THIS OF the moment he realized he wanted to marry me. First, he thought, *I want to marry this girl.* And then he thought: *Oh shit.*

The moment he had his *Oh shit* epiphany, I was alone in the shower, singing loudly and tragically off-key. It's a sad fact that though I love to sing, I'm not at all good at it. I'm reasonably sure I was singing "Cool Rider" from *Grease 2* (the far superior Grease movie). Something about my terrible singing sent love bubbles dancing from his eyes.

Why the *Oh shit*? Because my husband is Korean American and I am not. Not only am I not Korean American, I am Jamaican American, which is to say that I'm black. He thought *Oh shit* because in that moment he could foresee the trouble that loving and marrying me would cause in his family.

I was pretty naïve back then. We were both twenty-eight years old and in graduate school studying creative writing. It truly didn't occur to me that anyone would object to us being together. My parents didn't. It didn't even occur to me that they might.

A year after that singing-in-the-shower moment, my husband-to-be proposed. By that time we'd been through a lot with his family.

When he first told them that we were dating, they threatened to disown him. It scared him so much that we broke up for twelve hours. Back then my husband was the kind of wonderful son who called his mother once a week. After we started dating, those phone calls dried up. Why? Because every phone call became a lecture on why we shouldn't be dating. And what were the stated reasons? *You have nothing in common. Korean culture and black culture don't mix. She will disgrace our family. What will happen to your children? Black people are . . . less.*

After we got engaged, his parents did disown him. This really happened. It broke his heart and it broke mine. I'm certain it broke his mother's as well. I don't think she wanted to do it, but she somehow felt she had to. I imagine that she thought the loss of his family would persuade him to do what she saw as the right thing.

And then came his brother's wedding. As his fiancée I was, of course, invited. Also, his brother and his wife had been nothing but supportive from the very beginning. They insisted that I attend. But I knew if I attended, his parents would not. I made the choice to stay away because I didn't want to ruin the day for my future brother- and sister-in-law. I still believe I did the right thing. But I am conspicuously missing from those family photos. My husband and I still notice my absence.

Aside from his parents, there are some other challenges to being an interracial couple. These days he and I still get a lot of curious glances. When I put a jar of kimchi into my grocery cart at our favorite Korean grocery store, Korean people stare. When he picks up a can of ackee at the Jamaican store, Jamaican people stare. We get the occasional snide remark from both sides. When we have oysters at our favorite date-night spot, white people stare. One of our white friends jokingly says that this is because my husband and I are two different kinds of nonwhite.

Two years after we married, we moved to Los Angeles. With her son so close to home again, his mother made contact. It would take another year before I was invited to her house, and then only if his father was not there. It would be another eight years before I was invited with his father present.

At various times over the years, my husband has considered breaking all contact with his parents. I'm the one who has persuaded him not to. I thought we could find a place—a narrow island of understanding—where his parents wouldn't have to lose a son and a son wouldn't have to lose his parents. Luckily, we did find that island. Of course, our relationship with his parents is not what it could be. There's a part of my heart and a part of his that is guarded against them. But, having said that, our relationship with them is good. I say this without hesitation or reservation. As complicated as it is, I love his parents. I'm sure they love me. I'm sure they love our daughter.

Are my family and I the exception to their *black people are less* rule? Definitely.

Are they still racist? Again, definitely.

Still, though, something inside of them has shifted. Maybe it's just exposure—years of interaction because of birthdays and school functions and *Chuseok* dinners. Maybe it's witnessing just how much their son loves me. Maybe it's witnessing how much I love him. They are more open to the world than they were before I came into their lives.

And that counts for something.

That counts as hope.

One day, a few years after my husband and I were married, my mother asked me if all this drama and heartache was worth it. She was justifiably angry at my mother- and father-in-law.

Was it worth it? she asked me.

Of course it was.

It was then, and it is now. I would do it again a thousand times over. Because here's the thing: I am completely in love with my husband. I think he's the best thing ever—the bee's knees, the cat's meow, the milk *and* the crème. He's my best friend. He's my creative partner. He's a wonderful father. Together we made a kind, happy, beautiful little girl destined to make the world laugh. I won the love lottery when I met him. I wouldn't give him up for something as fundamentally stupid, devoid of hope, and morally corrupt as racism. I wouldn't give him up for anything.

HOPE NATION

DAVID LEVITHAN   LIBBA BRAY   ANGIE THOMAS
ALLY CONDIE   MARIE LU   JEFF ZENTNER
NICOLA YOON   **KATE HART**   GAYLE FORMAN
CHRISTINA DIAZ GONZALEZ   ATIA ABAWI
ALEX LONDON   HOWARD BRYANT   ALLY CARTER
ROMINA GARBER   RENÉE AHDIEH   AISHA SAEED
JENNY TORRES SANCHEZ   NIC STONE
JULIE MURPHY   I. W. GREGORIO   JAMES DASHNER
JASON REYNOLDS   BRENDAN KIELY

KATE HART

Wings and Teeth

IT'S A WEEK BEFORE MY deadline. I've had months to write this essay.

I'm still staring at a blank page.

My task is to write something about hope, something inspiring and honest. But the problem is that I have a combative relationship with the concept. Optimism, faith, whatever you want to call it—hope as an abstract idea has always just felt flimsy. I associate it with Hallmark cards and motivational speakers, with Facebook click-bait and vague platitudes like "Everything happens for a reason" or "When a door closes, a window opens." According to Emily Dickinson, it's "the thing with feathers," flitting about and singing.

But trying to take on the world's challenges with nothing but well-meaning sentiments feels like wearing flip-flops to a bar fight or trying to get comfortable in a hammock tied between two drinking straws. Don't get me wrong—I've always felt the draw of giving your worries over to an outside force. But I'm also an agnostic whose brain demands logic and refuses to put its eggs in unseen baskets. I often feel like two people: the idealist who wants to look on the bright side, and the pragmatist who sits on her shoulder reminding everyone that reality is a construct and we'll all die in the end.

My shoulder cynic. She's fun at parties.

I decide to take a walk to clear my head. My husband and my dog come along, as well as, unfortunately, my shoulder cynic. "You know," she says as I get ready, "for someone who claims not to believe in the unseen, it's pretty weird that you always put your right shoe on first."

I blush. She's right—it's a completely illogical habit, but for some reason, at some point in childhood, I decided that putting my left shoe on first would bring death and destruction to all I love. Because . . . logic. "It's not like it hurts anyone," I tell her. "I don't force anyone else to put their shoes on the same way."

Shoulder Cynic snorts. "I'm just saying, superstitions make even less sense than religion, yet you put your hopes in them."

"Not hopes," I argue. "Just comfort. I know full well that it's dumb."

"If you say so," she says, and we head outside.

The sun is setting as we start the one-mile trek around our neighborhood. Lightning bugs blink in the dusk, much more attractive than their bloodsucking mosquito relatives. I slap at the latter as I tell my husband, "Maybe you should write this essay."

"Me?" he says.

"You're the one who gave the inspirational graduation speech." With a purple mortarboard atop his long hair, my then-boyfriend encouraged our classmates to stay idealistic and never give in to the creeping pessimism of adulthood. The hair has been cut since, but his optimism remains intact. "I was already cynical when you gave it," I say. "I just admired your approach."

"That's why we're a good team," he replies. "We balance each other out."

"I'm not sure 'marry someone who counteracts your natural Eeyore tendencies' is a great thesis."

A rabbit runs across the road in front of us, and we both say "Bunny!" Bunny sightings are considered good luck in our household—a less morbid version of the traditional rabbit's foot. Rabbit roadkill, on the other hand, ruins my entire day. In my heart, I know seeing bunnies in springtime, whether dead or alive, is a statistical likelihood, not an indication of the universe's favor. But spotting them in the yard still feels encouraging.

"You know what we call that, right?" whispers Shoulder Cynic.

"No," I whisper back. "Hope requires conviction. I just like bunnies."

Throughout college, when I had trouble with a paper, I'd find a quote to use as a backbone, adding arguments along its sides like ribs. Finding an epigraph to help with this essay makes sense. "Maybe I can use the Dickinson line?" I say. "'Hope is the thing with feathers . . .'"

"'That perches in the soul,'" my Shoulder Cynic goes on. Unlike the shoulder devils of cartoons, she's neither red nor has a pointy tail. But she does have horns sprouting through her spiky hair. "'And sings the tune,'" she says, "and blah blah blah, something about keeping you warm."

"Ugh. I thought I was on to something."

"That's what we call 'false hopes.'"

I pause. "False hopes might be a plan, actually." She watches as I start fact checking what I think I know about Doomtree, a "great band you don't know (but should)" according to *Time* magazine. The group is a seven-member collective that makes albums together but also functions as a label, merchandiser, and even publisher, and several of their early releases were called "False Hopes."

Though I'm fairly sure that I know the origins of that title, I decide to tweet at member Dessa, who's one of my particular favorites.

```
@kate_hart: I'm writing an essay about hope for
an anthology & wanted to reference DTR's "False
Hopes"—could swear I saw an (1/2)
@kate_hart: (2/2) interview where you explained
the title was bc all art is a false hope? But
maybe hallucinated it. Can you point me in the
right direction?
@dessadarling: Not me I'm afraid. That series
existed before I joined the crew—@CECILOTTER13's
idea, I think.
```

"Even your False Hopes were false hopes," Shoulder Cynic says.

"You're a riot." I add Cecil Otter to the search, which just reveals that False Hopes was the name of his pre-Doomtree band—a group that, in his words, "didn't do anything." The new crew considered using the same name, then kicked around other ideas, including

Seven Bums, Seven Trees, Doom Bums . . . and Doom Hope. "Doom Hope," I repeat.

"Well," says Shoulder Cynic, "that's cheery."

"I'll admit I expected a better story."

She snickers, pointing at the screen. Dessa goes on to tell the interviewer that if the naming story is a disappointment, fans should know that the band started finding so many dead birds outside their shared house that they put a dead-bird drawing on their merchandise.

"I guess False Hopes are things with feathers too," Shoulder Cynic says.

"Hilarious." I click through a few items in their store and pause on the familiar "wings and teeth" logo. "Maybe I can use this."

"Don't count on it."

The logo doubles as a hand sign that fans throw at shows, so the crew has been asked about it in multiple interviews. In one, Cecil claims that dental records are used to identify the dead, and the logo was "sort of a morbid idea. The idea that we are supposed to make something lasting."

"That's pretty good, right?" I say. "Art is made in hopes of being remembered."

"Or . . ." Shoulder Cynic points to another interview and reads out loud. "Paper Tiger said 'it's supposed to look gnarly and get your attention.'"

That's not very inspirational. Nor is Dessa's follow-up, reminiscing that a former band member drew the logo after a little too much Budweiser and a joke about a tooth with wings.

"Well, it's not a total loss," I say. "Maybe the lesson is that you never know where important things will come from. Sometimes accidents turn out happy. Sometimes your dumb name and drunk joke logo still manage to inspire other artists for a decade."

"Or sometimes you just have a crappy essay."

"Sometimes," I admit.

The next morning, I find my sons eating breakfast in the kitchen. "I need your help," I tell them. "What gives you hope for the future?"

"Bakeries," my nine-year-old replies without pause.

"The development of hyperloops," says my eleven-year-old.

I'm in serious trouble.

The idea of accidental inspiration sticks with me, though. It turns out that lots of things were discovered or created by chance. Penicillin, for example, was discovered when a scientist left his dirty petri dishes in the sink. The mold that grew on them ate the germs he'd been working with, and voila: measles, mumps, polio, and lots of other diseases became almost extinct. A petri dish mistake also brought us the color mauve, inadvertently resulting in the world's first synthetic dye. Saccharin was discovered because a scientist forgot to wash his hands and noticed dinner was unusually sweet. Nitrous oxide was being used as a party drug in the 1800s until the inventor's friend injured himself without pain and they realized anesthesia could be a big thing.

Both chewing gum and Silly Putty were supposed to be a replacement for rubber. Velcro was inspired by burrs sticking to a dog after a hike. Play-Doh was originally created to clean wallpaper in coal-heated houses. Safety glass, Popsicles, Post-it Notes, the Slinky, Super Glue, cornflakes, and Vaseline were all happy accidents that turned into useful products.

Of course, there's an argument to be made that none of those discoveries were entirely accidental—they were a matter of someone paying attention with an open mind and seeing new possibilities. Maybe that's how we'll get the hyperloops my oldest wants.

"Your essay, on the other hand," Shoulder Cynic pipes up. Somehow she's managed to get headphones over her horns, but she takes them off just to argue with me.

"I have another idea," I assure her. "I'm going to crib from Badass Ladies." One of my favorite side projects is an interview series called Badass Ladies You Should Know.

"Which no one reads!" she crows.

I ignore her. The website has a hashtag for badass ladies in history, and it should be easy to find examples. Three hours later, I have a long list of historical trailblazers: "Stagecoach Mary" Fields, the first female African American mail carrier in the United States; Noor Inayat Khan, a secret agent during World War II; Bertha Parker Pallan, the first female Native American archaeologist; Madam C. J. Walker, black cosmetics maker and the first self-made millionaire in the United States; pioneering trans activist Marsha "Pay It No Mind" Johnson; Chickasaw dancer Te Ata; early Appalachian Trail hiker Emma Gatewood; architect Zaha Hadid; inventor of rock-and-roll Sister Rosetta Tharpe—all these amazing women . . .

"That we've never heard of, just like Doomtree." The problem is that Shoulder Cynic has the same history degree I do. "Women are always written out of history and they always will be."

"Then how did we hear about these?" I demand.

"Some records are bound to survive. But think of all the ones that didn't."

Disheartened, I turn back to my screen. *History is written by the victors* is hardly a new concept, and I have to admit that even these women's stories are cobbled together largely from records curated by men. Still . . . "It doesn't have to be so all-or-nothing," I tell her. "You can find encouragement in the progress that's been made without ignoring that there's more work to be done."

"Yeah, well." Shoulder Cynic points to another tab that's open on my laptop. "It's a hell of a lot of work."

"I'm not getting distracted by Twitter right now." But I still click the tab. Unsurprisingly, the news is full of terrible stories: corruption and war, violence against people of color, regulations on whom we can love. A major review outlet is panning a colleague's book for not portraying assault victims in a way they deem acceptable. A formerly beloved celebrity who admitted to rape has escaped justice. A huge storm is building in the gulf, yet another child has fallen victim to an unsecured gun, and a Facebook acquaintance has cancer and can't afford treatment while another is trying to sell me overpriced leggings.

"You know what it reminds me of?" asks Shoulder Cynic. "That protest sign that says 'I can't believe we still have to protest this crap!'"

"Maybe that'll be the epigraph." I look up examples and laugh sadly. The slogan itself is nothing new—there are pictures of it dating back to at least 2004. "Or maybe it'll be my epitaph. I guess history does repeat itself."

Doomtree may not be rolling in dough, but they're making a living from their art. I'm just making a little pocket change from mine, and later that afternoon, I have some Etsy orders to finish.

Woodworking is a new hobby, but I learned fiber arts from many women in my family, especially my grandma. She primarily used acrylics, but Grandma was always exploring new mediums, and her Dallas apartment was filled with art supplies. She also worked full-time managing the complex, and lived next door to the pool, the combination of which ate up enough of our time together that she never got to teach me stained glass or painting or dollhouse furniture making.

Grandma came down with early-onset Alzheimer's when I was in my late teens, and passed away when I was twenty-six. She never found success as an artist. Her works don't hang in galleries, and art books mention her only as a muse to her more successful brother.

But I have one of her paintings and a piece of glass to remember her by—her version of wings and teeth, I suppose. I wonder what my own art will say. So far, it mostly says inappropriate words in embroidery and wooden signs.

"And a bunch of cheesy affirmations," Shoulder Cynic says.

"Har, har," I say, putting down the packing tape. "It's not like my art is all flowers and rainbows."

"Some of it is."

"Pride rainbows are different."

She rolls her eyes. "Pride rainbows are the *hopiest* of hope."

Fair point. "Well, maybe it's okay to spread a little hope even if you don't keep a lot for yourself."

"Like a do-it-yourself project."

"Exactly."

She rolls her eyes. "You're hopeless."

I'm stuck on the idea of false hope and hypocrisy. Maybe I don't think there's treasure at the end of the rainbow, but I can still appreciate that light and water vapor come together to make something beautiful.

I shudder to think how cheesy Shoulder Cynic would find that idea, so I keep searching for a different approach . . . which could also be called mindlessly scrolling through Instagram. I come across a picture of Dessa in a roomful of kids who are all flashing the wings and teeth sign. "Wow," I say, reading the caption. "I wish Dessa had come to *my* classroom to teach creative writing."

"It's cool that she gives back to the community," Shoulder Cynic admits. "I guess that's part of that whole scene, though." The Twin Cities have a flourishing music culture, anchored by the legacy of Prince's success and generosity. Though I grew up dancing around the house to my mom's vinyl copy of *1999,* I didn't realize until a few years ago just how influential that region has been when it comes to music.

"Tell them you found out through *Twilight!*" Shoulder Cynic demands.

I roll my eyes. "Why do you hate fun?"

To my surprise, she doesn't answer. I guess she thought I'd be embarrassed, but the fact is that *Twilight* changed my life. Really. Up to that point, I'd fancied myself a connoisseur of literature, despite the fact that Stephen King and Jean Auel and Dean Koontz made me a reader. When all of my girlfriends started reading Stephenie Meyer's series, I was full of disdain. I resisted no matter how much they tried to convince me the books were fun.

But then.

Our family took a camping trip to the National Seashore, and I decided I needed a "beach read," that condescending term for books that might otherwise be called "delightful" or "entertaining" or even "perceived as being for women." Naturally, I grabbed the "trashiest" read possible: a paperback copy full of sparkling vampires and love-struck teenagers.

Which I promptly read in one afternoon.

And then drove half an hour into town to get the sequels.

"They don't even have fangs!" Shoulder Cynic interrupts. My shrug knocks her into the crook of my elbow. "And they don't drink blood!"

"So? There's still beheadings and stuff."

She extends a set of wings and flies back to my shoulder. "I'm just saying—"

"Where did you get those?" I interrupt.

"You tell me," she says, folding them in. Unlike a bat's, her wings are a kaleidoscope of colors, the edges fuzzy as if the artist forgot to finish their outline. "Maybe I'm the angel on your shoulder, not the devil."

"I don't believe in either one."

"You don't believe in physical manifestations of your own psyche either, but here I am. And I'm saying that I demand some teeth in my bloodsuckers."

"Fine," I tell her. "We'll reread Anne Rice. But the point is that *Twilight* made me see my own condescending and sexist beliefs about literature."

The series was my door into the wide variety of books being written under the young-adult label, and made me want to write some of my own. And most unexpectedly, it reconnected me to my love of music, an interest that had fallen by the wayside while my children were babies. One of my favorite songs on the *New Moon* sequel soundtrack was half credited to Bon Iver (which turned out to be a band, not a person with a bummer of a name). Its creative force, Justin Vernon, had been involved in lots of projects around the Twin Cities—including several that overlapped with members of Doomtree, plus many more from around the world. Improbably, *Twilight* led me to music that's inspired my books, my art, and even my travels, catching new favorite bands on tour.

"I doubt that Stephenie Meyer sat down to write her book hoping that someday, some white woman in Arkansas would fall in love with a rap group from Minnesota," Shoulder Cynic says.

"But that's the point," I said. "Doomtree is pretty small and *Twilight* was huge, but they've both been successful in a lot of ways. And it should give people hope that you never know what big effects your small efforts might have."

"Does that give you hope?" she asks.

"No," I admit. "It makes me nervous that I can't control all the consequences of my actions."

"But it's still a good thing."

"I think it can be."

She gives me the side eye and puts her headphones back on.

Now it's a challenge. Now I have to find a way to prove to my shoulder cynic that she's wrong. There has to be some kind of argument that proves that hope is more than just the thing with feathers. "And you know what?" I say out of nowhere.

She drops the book she's been reading. "Do we have to do this now? I just got to the part where Lestat—"

"Feathers aren't even weak," I tell her.

"Oooookay."

"I mean, they hold up things like . . . eagles," I say. "And . . . hawks. Owls! Condors!"

"Condors are almost extinct."

I ignore her. "And you know what else? Feathers are a sign of achievement!"

She raises an eyebrow. "What, like, 'Look at me, I grew these—'"

"No, like in Native cultures. You have to earn feathers through bravery or accomplishment. Headdresses are equivalent to medals."

"Fine," she says, lifting her book back to her face. "So sometimes hope is the thing with medals and a headdress."

"Gah!" I pick her up and set her on my desk so that I can pace around the room. The most obvious example occurs to me and I whirl around, shocked that I haven't used it yet. "But what about Obama?"

She eyes me over the book's purple cover. "Obama has feathers?"

"No, for the love . . ." I shake my head. "His whole campaign was based on hope. And he *won*. He got in the Oval Office as the first black president and had that quote put on the rug—remember? 'The moral arc of the universe is long, but it bends toward justice.'"

"Does it, though?" she asks.

"I mean, empirically speaking, no . . ."

"That's not even his quote," she says. "It's Martin Luther King Junior's. Look it up."

"I *know* that," I argue, but look anyway. To the surprise of my history nerd heart, the quote is neither Obama's nor King's: King actually paraphrased it from nineteenth-century abolitionist and minister Theodore Parker, who was also the author of the phrase *a government of all the people, by all the people, for all the people*. "Lincoln used that in the Gettysburg Address."

"And Parker didn't even get credit," Shoulder Cynic says.

"Yeah, but he's influenced two hundred years of the fight for civil rights since."

"Well," she says, examining her nails. They're bloodred, which seems a little over the top to me. At least try to be subtle. "Now we're just back to 'protesting this crap again.' We're still having the same fight."

"It's not *exactly* the same fight," I say. "And who are you to dismiss the work that got us this far?"

"That's deep," she says, and lights a clove cigarette. "Use that in your essay."

"Fine!" I yell. "You win, okay! There's no hope but a fool's hope! Frodo would never really have reached Mount Doom! Voldemort would have won! All we have is Doom Hope and a crappy essay!"

"The problem," she says, blowing a smoke ring to rival Gandalf's, "is that you don't really believe that."

"No. I don't." I take a few deep breaths. "What I've really concluded is that hope isn't some frail thing with feathers that needs loving care and a strong cage. What I really think is that hope is in the work. That it lives in the space between what's been done and what could be accomplished. And I think—" I take another break to collect my thoughts. "I think you're missing the larger point. History isn't a closed story. We're still part of it. Parker and King and Obama and all those badass ladies didn't fail—they reached several stops on the way to their destination. You have to have the small successes to create the large ones. And in order to reach even the small goals, you can't just sit back and wait for rabbit's feet or untied shoes to get you there. You have to put in the work and recognize that even your greatest effort is only going to be part of a much larger whole—and that's okay."

Shoulder Cynic watches me, waiting to see if I'm finished, then gives me a slow clap. "So what you're saying is that hope can't just have feathers. It needs wings." She expands hers, and smiles, revealing two large fangs I've never seen before.

I laugh. "And teeth. Blood and wings and teeth."

She flits up my arm to see my laptop screen. "Looks like your essay finally has some too."

I crane my neck to look at her. "You mean all this time . . . I thought you were—"

"You're welcome," she says, but she doesn't go perch in my soul. She just gets herself comfortable on my shoulder for next time.

References:

"About I Doomtree." DTR. Accessed June 14, 2017. http://www.doomtree.net/about/.

Bernard, Adam. "Doomtree Interview." RapReview Feature for August 12, 2008—Doomtree Interview. August 12, 2008. Accessed June 14, 2017. http://www.rapreviews.com/interview/doomtree08.html.

"The opera-loving sisters who 'stumbled' into heroism." BBC News. January 28, 2017. Accessed June 14, 2017. http://www.bbc.com/news/uk-england-tyne-38732779.

http://www.listenupdenver.com/8821/doomtree-talks-no-kings-and-their-famous-wings-and-teeth-logo/

http://list25.com/25-accidental-inventions-that-changed-the-world/3/

https://www.poets.org/poetsorg/poem/hope-thing-feathers-254

HOPE NATION

DAVID LEVITHAN   LIBBA BRAY   ANGIE THOMAS
ALLY CONDIE   MARIE LU   JEFF ZENTNER
NICOLA YOON   KATE HART   **GAYLE FORMAN**
CHRISTINA DIAZ GONZALEZ   ATIA ABAWI
ALEX LONDON   HOWARD BRYANT   ALLY CARTER
ROMINA GARBER   RENÉE AHDIEH   AISHA SAEED
JENNY TORRES SANCHEZ   NIC STONE
JULIE MURPHY   I. W. GREGORIO   JAMES DASHNER
JASON REYNOLDS   BRENDAN KIELY

GAYLE FORMAN

Shot of Hope

TWELVE WEEKS BEFORE MY HUSBAND and I were due to leave for a yearlong trip around the globe, the world changed. On a clear, sunny, almost sadistically beautiful late-summer day, a group of terrorists hijacked and weaponized four airplanes. The rest is now history.

Back then, I lived in Manhattan, a few miles north of Ground Zero, close enough for the smoke from the smoldering fires to permeate everything. Sometimes smoke has a nice aroma, of campfires and woodstoves and innocence. Not this smoke. It reeked of something caustic, chemical, toxic, a physical manifestation of hatred that seeped into your clothes, your pores, your heart.

I was a journalist at the time, so it was my job to use my press pass to gain entry to the cordoned-off streets near Ground Zero and interview people, to get them to explain the inexplicable. Instead, I just wandered the ash-covered eerily empty blocks, unable to speak to anyone, looking so dazed and upset that rescue workers confused me for someone directly impacted by the attacks and offered me the support of service dogs. I felt a little like a fraud. I hadn't been anywhere near the towers when the planes hit (I was four miles uptown, watching a VHS recording of *An Affair to Remember*, a favorite movie I haven't been able to watch since), and I hadn't lost a loved one. I didn't know anyone who worked at Cantor Fitzgerald. I wasn't related to any firefighter, let alone one of the 343 who'd lost their lives that day.

But I was grieving. For my city. For my country. And for myself.

My husband worked for a major news network, and like all of the networks, it was running twenty-four-hour coverage of the attacks. So he was always at the office. I couldn't bear to be alone in our apartment. I started going with him to work at night, even though by then someone had sent poisonous anthrax to the building and the lobby was now full of workers in hazmat suits. They looked like Martians. Like people from a world I no longer recognized.

My husband often worked the graveyard shift—a fitting name, because everything seemed like a graveyard then—so I would make a bed on one of the desks or lie down on the floor and fall asleep as the mounted televisions around me endlessly played those weirdly cinematic images of the planes going into the towers, or the surreal and elegiac moment when the towers imploded upon themselves. In between the shots of fiery special-effects-worthy destruction, they showed the sobbing relatives, clutching the missing-person fliers that would become the wallpaper of the city. And then there were the endless parades of talking heads, warning us about a danger that had been in plain sight all this time. They showed images of bearded men half a world away who despised us, our way of life, who wanted to destroy us.

Beware, the TV told us. *The world has changed. Danger is everywhere.*

It was not a time without hope. In fact, in New York City, strangers blanketed fire stations with flowers, with casseroles. We asked one another on the streets if everything was okay. We gathered in parks to sing songs: "Amazing Grace," "I Will Survive," and "New York, New York," the only hymns we knew.

This buoyed me, but still, I was scared and despairing. The world out there had just announced its hatred. And I was supposed to travel out of my cocoon and into its maw? For an entire year?

I was already on shaky ground. Seven months earlier, I had lost my two best friends and their two young children in a car accident on a snowy Oregon road. A month after that, while I was still stumbling around in a haze of shock and grief, another friend contracted what seemed like food poisoning after an office potluck and then grew quickly and acutely ill, dying a week later. (Much later, I learned he suffered from a chronic illness that weakened his immune system.)

There's a maxim about young people thinking they're invincible, taking incredible risks because they believe themselves impervious to death or disease or danger. I was never one of those young people. Although I wasn't exactly cautious, I always understood, at least hypothetically, that the angel of death was never far off. But after my friends died, the wall between life and death—which was always only illusory anyway—vanished, taking with it some of my abiding hope that things would, one way or another, be okay.

And then 9/11 happened. And I began to wonder if anything would ever be okay again.

•   •   •

I started traveling when I was seven, when my parents took my siblings and me on a six-week trip through Europe and the Middle East, including a week in what was then a very Communist Romania. We couldn't afford a new car, but we could afford to travel. It set a precedent. Experience was more valuable than things. Travel was the most important education of all.

When I was sixteen, I went away to a small town in England to study abroad for a year because somehow, even though I'd never really been away on my own, I decided this was a good idea. My rationale at the time had something to do with my love of British New Wave bands—of which, in the tiny village of five hundred where I landed, there were exactly zero—but really, I think I was bearing the fruit of the seeds my parents had planted. That travel was the best education possible.

And it was. I learned so much that year. I studied psychology and sociology, I learned to play guitar and edit a newspaper, I began writing a novel, I marched against nuclear proliferation and apartheid. I learned that people could seem very different from you—and in 1986, people in the Midlands of England basically spoke a different language and did things that I found bizarre, like sharing their bathwater and never showing emotion—but really the differences were just window dressing covering the human heart. I learned I could make deep friendships, take risks, survive homesickness and loneliness and heartbreak. I learned that maybe I was braver than I'd thought. Which in turn made me braver yet.

After the year abroad, I came home and told my parents I wasn't going to college once I graduated. I would be attending the University of Life. (They couldn't argue. They were the ones who'd taught me about the importance of travel.) After I finished my senior year, I bought a one-way ticket and a rail pass and set off, with no particular plan, but a growing flicker of hope that if I opened myself up to the world, it would receive me in kind.

I traveled for four months and then settled in Amsterdam, where I knew no one. Strangers offered me a room in their squat. Offered to teach me to speak Dutch and cooked me dinners. I got a job as a maid in a hotel. I learned the language. I found a flat. I met people from everywhere—Ireland, Israel, Surinam, Morocco. I met prostitutes and political refugees. At first they seemed different, and then, as I got to know them, not.

When I finally went to college three years later, I decided to become a journalist, primarily because it was a job that would allow me to keep seeing the world (before journalism, I'd considered becoming a flight attendant). By then, I was addicted to traveling. Not because it was easy. I often trekked alone and on a bare-bones budget. I broke out in hives in the middle of Belgium. I got terrible strep throat in Poland. I spent a terrible night in a stuffy room in Turkey, throwing up from food poisoning. I was often lonely, too cold, too hot, tired, uncomfortable. I had my backpack stolen. My heart broken. My patience tested.

And yet, I loved it. I loved meeting new people who seemed, initially, foreign, different, and then passing through some invisible barrier and seeing that our differences weren't so great after all. I loved being intimidated by a new place, a new culture—okay, I didn't love that part—and then a few days later, becoming less intimidated, and then comfortable.

After college, I spent twelve years as magazine journalist, traveling around to increasingly intimidating places—Northern Ireland, Sierra Leone, Pakistan—and meeting people seemingly different from me, and becoming ever more convinced that though our languages might vary, our cultures might seem irreconcilable, and our religions might be at odds, our similarities were greater than our differences. The people I met wanted to be loved and give love. They wanted their communities to be safe. They wanted better lives for their families. They wanted to be part of something larger than themselves. They wanted to believe in a better world.

Nearly every person I have ever met—from the child soldier to the refugee mother—shared these traits. Probably you do too.

Experienced a traveler as I am, I still get nervous before a trip. I can't sleep. I cry for inexplicable reasons. I imagine worst-case scenarios all the time (it's actually a handy trait for a novelist, less so for a traveler). Each time I fling myself into some new place, encounter a new culture, a new language, a new currency, a new landscape, a new cuisine, I am convinced something, or everything, will go terribly awry.

Proving myself wrong is the core of why I love to travel. Each time I am embraced and helped or allowed to help and to embrace, I remember all over again. I can choose to see people as others, as threats. Or I can choose to see them as essentially human. I choose the latter and am rewarded every time.

This is why I travel. Not to see museums or beaches or sunsets. But to receive a booster shot of hope.

•   •   •

The attacks on 9/11 seemed to be a repudiation of my beliefs, or so the people on TV kept telling me. The world was dangerous. People were different. The warmth I'd experienced was two-faced. My faith was misplaced. The shot of hope was actually a poison pill.

My husband and I talked about canceling the trip.

As the days went on, we learned that as we had been meticulously planning our flights—Tonga, New Zealand, Hong Kong, Bangkok, New Delhi, Nairobi—a group of terrorists had been meticulously plotting much shorter flights. We learned that as we were grieving in New York City, people half a world away were cheering. We learned that battle lines had been drawn. Enemies we didn't even know we had were unmasked. The destinations that had seemed so exciting to us before—not just the places on the round-the-world ticket we'd bought but the places we planned to go in between, like Kazakhstan and Yemen and Zanzibar—seemed, from the TV at least, like cauldrons of hatred and danger.

I wanted to cancel. I was scared. After the year I'd had, hope seemed in short supply. And I didn't want to cancel. Because after the year I'd had, I needed hope more than ever.

Spoiler: We went.

That year abroad wasn't perfect. I fought with my husband, a lot. I got sick in China, again in India, and once more in France. I missed my friends from home. I missed my routine. I missed having a sense of purpose. But all in all, it was a wonderful year and, maybe more important, a healing one. Because in spite of the terrible things I'd seen on TV, in the markets, the bazaars, the plazas, the mountains, the back alleys, the tea shops, the world remained much as it had been. It had its share of bad people, its share of scammers, but they were the exceptions. Mostly people were as I'd always encountered them: kind, generous, willing to show visitors respect and sometimes even love.

I met a whole new crop of strangers who became friends. Visited a whole new lot of intimidating places that became, if not home, then home away from home. I got scared plenty of times, often when boarding a plane to the next place that according to the news was on the verge of catastrophe. But aside from the times I was in a minibus or taxi, taking a steep curve at sixty miles an hour, I never thought I was in danger.

Maybe this was because as a white American, I had that privilege. I was traveling on a shoestring budget, but I had an emergency credit card that could whisk me out of a truly dicey situation, an American passport that would allow me safe haven to many places. I am well aware, particularly at this point in time, that this is a luxury not shared by all.

But maybe it was because I wasn't really in danger. On TV, terrible things continued to happen. New terrorist threats. A buildup to a war. But on the ground, in the places I was visiting, it was just people, who were sometimes bad but mostly good, getting on with life.

• • •

The year abroad gave me hope at a time when I needed it most. Not because everything was perfect. The world has never been perfect. Conflict is woven into our history just as much as progress. There have always been men who believe the righteousness of their ideals justifies no end of violence. There have always been leaders who foment fear to solidify their power.

But the year showed me that healing was possible. That even in the face of devastation, there was renewal. And that people were as I had believed them to be. Not perfect, but trying to be better. Kind of like me.

Perhaps most important, the year showed me that no matter what happened, no matter how large the devastation or grief, life went on.

Life goes on.

Fifteen years pass since 9/11, since our trip. One terror group is replaced by another. Grim headlines continue. I have two children. I change careers. The world becomes wary, then angry.

Though I travel a lot for work, I haven't undertaken one of those big, fling-yourself-into-adventure trips. Not because the world has grown more dangerous—though the TV and Internet would have you believe otherwise—but because I had children, and the prospect of globe-trotting with them as ornery youngsters was a terror I could never overcome.

But in 2016 my husband and I decided it was time and began

planning a big trip with the whole family: England, France, Israel, the West Bank, Ethiopia, and Kenya for the following summer.

Our itinerary was like a Where's Waldo of trouble spots. England, which in 2017 alone saw the bombing at the Ariana Grande concert in Manchester and the van attack on London Bridge. Paris, which has been the site of several attacks over the last few years. Israel, a hotbed of unrest, and the West Bank, if you believe the media reports, a hive of suicide bombers. Ethiopia, which was under a state of emergency, and Kenya, which the State Department warned us we probably should not visit.

If the world looked bleak on TV in 2001, it looked like Doom according to TV, websites, and Twitter now. I had a moment of doubt. Had things really changed this time? Had humanity gone off? My kids were only nine and thirteen. Was I pushing them into harm's way because I was itchy to dust off my backpack? Because I wanted to teach them a lesson, about the importance of travel? Because I wanted to prove to them—or re-prove to myself—that fear is not a foregone conclusion but a decision? Because I was desperate to believe that in spite of the dispiriting headlines, the attacks that now seemed so commonplace were still exceptional, the people who perpetrated them outliers whose terrible deeds were exaggerated by traditional and social media and by leaders bent on stoking fear? Because I wanted them to understand that the world broadcast on TV was a distortion, about as accurate a portrayal of how human beings live as, say, the Kardashians?

And even if this was a lesson I wanted to impart, did I have to drag them halfway around the world? After all, you don't need to get a passport to understand the disconnect between the world on

TV or the Internet and the actual world in which human beings dwell. You simply need to turn off the screen, step outside your comfort zone, your bubble, to go to a new neighborhood for a walk or a new church for services, to talk to someone different from you. To breathe through that moment of fear and uncertainty and come out the other side.

In the end, dear reader, we went traveling. Because I wanted to introduce my girls to the world as I believed it and because it was time for them to start receiving their hope inoculations (along with those for typhoid and yellow fever they had to get before we left).

It's a strong shot of medicine. The boosters I've gotten through the years of travel stay with me, swim through my blood, remind me, with every grim headline, that though the world seems to be changing in dizzying, disheartening ways, it remains, in some essential way, as I've always known it. It gives me the strength to breathe through the fear, to cross over to the other side.

The other side is where hope lives.

DAVID LEVITHAN   LIBBA BRAY   ANGIE THOMAS
ALLY CONDIE   MARIE LU   JEFF ZENTNER
NICOLA YOON   KATE HART   GAYLE FORMAN
CHRISTINA DIAZ GONZALEZ   ATIA ABAWI
ALEX LONDON   HOWARD BRYANT   ALLY CARTER
ROMINA GARBER   RENÉE AHDIEH   AISHA SAEED
JENNY TORRES SANCHEZ   NIC STONE
JULIE MURPHY   I. W. GREGORIO   JAMES DASHNER
JASON REYNOLDS   BRENDAN KIELY

CHRISTINA DIAZ GONZALEZ

Baseball Pasta

IT WAS A WARM SUMMER evening, and the sun was sinking past the horizon, creating a swirl of bright pink, orange, and purple streaks in the sky. The red clay of the infield was framed by the tall chain-link fence that separated the bleachers from the players, and the lights had already come on. Farther in the distance, past the outfield, were the pine trees that covered most of the county. Those trees were our town's claim to fame . . . We were the Pine Tree Capital of the South. A pulp and paper mill town where most people were, in one way or another, connected to the mill . . . including my family. My dad's job was the reason I was born in Perry . . . the only Hispanic girl in that small North Florida town.

The crowd cheered as the ballplayers took the field. My mother waved to my dad, the third baseman, and he smiled and tugged the rim of his cap. My grandfather had already taken his regular spot along the fence while the players started their warm-ups. It was the church softball league, and the players were the fathers, brothers, and sons of the people in the stands. The game would soon start, and I couldn't have cared less.

Although that hadn't always been the case.

At one point, I dreamed of being the first girl on the team, but that idea quickly ended when I misjudged a fast pitch and got whacked in the head. And that happened when I was just playing catch with my dad in the backyard! Earning that golf-ball-sized bump on my forehead made me realize that playing softball was not for me, but my dad still insisted I learn about every sport. So, there I was, sitting on the bleachers next to my mother, little sister, and grandmother, getting ready to cheer for Leo's Lions. My little sister was even wearing her Leo's Cubs shirt, but I thought myself way too cool for that sort of thing. Instead, I had on my light pink T-shirt with a glittery rainbow painted across the front.

"*Hoy voy a gritar como los Americanos*," Abi, my grandmother, whispered as she leaned closer to me.

My eyebrows scrunched together. What did she mean, she was going to yell like the Americans? What was my grandmother up to?

"Abi . . ." My voice quivered a little. I had an uneasy feeling about this.

But she brushed off my concern. She told me in Spanish that she'd been paying attention during the games and that, although she didn't understand why the fans liked pasta so much, she was going to join in the cheering this time.

Pasta? At a ball game?

Now I was really confused. What could she have possibly heard to make her think that people talked about pasta during a baseball game? The only things they sold here were hot dogs, Cracker Jack, and candy.

"Hey, Christina!" a voice in the distance interrupted my thoughts.

My friend Angela was standing by the concession stand, waving at me. She was next to several of my classmates, and I could tell *that* was the place to be.

Thoughts of my grandmother, pasta, and baseball disappeared as the more pressing thoughts of being with my friends took over. "Mami, I'm going to hang out with my friends for a while, okay?" I scooted toward the edge of the bleachers to make my quick getaway.

"I want to go too!" my little sister declared.

I widened my eyes at my mom, silently begging her not to make me bring her along. Three-year-olds did not mix well with the sophistication of middle schoolers.

"Not today," my mom told her, "but Christina will bring back some Cracker Jack for you." She gave me a wink.

"Thank you," I mouthed as she handed my grandmother a dollar to pass to me.

"*Ten cuidado*," my grandmother said, reminding me to be careful as if walking around the baseball field might somehow be dangerous. Then again, she also wanted me to always wear a sweater if there was even the slightest evening breeze, so it wasn't an unusual request, coming from her.

I gave a small wave in acknowledgment, jumped off the bleachers, and hit the ground running.

By the time I returned with a half-eaten box of Cracker Jack, the game was about to start. My plan was to drop off the snack and then run back to spend the rest of the game with my friends.

As I was handing the box to my sister, the loudspeaker crackled.

"Please stand for our national anthem," the announcer said.

On the field the players from both teams were already lined up, their caps over their hearts.

As the first few notes of "The Star-Spangled Banner" played, everyone in the stands stood up and put their hands on their chests. There was no way I could leave now. It would be a sign of disrespect to the country that had welcomed my family when their own country had been lost. I could see my grandfather no longer slouching against the fence, but standing straight and facing the flag that flapped in the distance.

As the music ended and the crowd clapped, the announcer called out, "Play ball!"

That was my sign to take off. But before I could make a clean getaway, Abi grabbed my arm.

"*Mira*," she said. *Watch.*

I froze. It was too late to stop her.

She cupped her hands around her mouth and shouted . . . "LINGUINE!"

Linguine? The pasta? That's what my grandmother, with her heavy Cuban accent, had decided to shout at the start of a baseball game?

In retrospect, it shouldn't have surprised me that she wanted to participate in the game. My grandmother was not one to sit quietly on the sidelines. She loved life and believed you had to act in order to shape your own destiny. It was obvious from her life experiences.

Abi didn't understand or speak much English, but living in a town where no one spoke Spanish never slowed her down. She had a smile for everyone and a loving embrace for those she knew. There was an attitude about her that said anything could be overcome . . . with hope and action. "*Haz bien y no mires a quien,*" she used to tell me, which loosely translates to "Do good and don't worry who it's for." It was one of her life mottos, and it was something she expected us all to live by as well.

When she was younger, Abi had lived a relatively easy upper-middle-class life. That all changed with the Communist Cuban Revolution of 1959.

Cuba, the country she loved, quickly changed. The false promises of helping the poor and social equality came at a great cost. Private property was confiscated for government use. Newspapers were shut down. Freedom of the press was outlawed. And anyone speaking against the government could be arrested or, worse, sent to the *paredon* . . . the firing wall. Just like that, fundamental rights disappeared under the guise of the revolution.

Within months, my grandmother saw government soldiers take the homes and businesses my grandparents and so many others had worked hard to create. She witnessed the loss of friends and family as some turned against her, depending on where they stood politically. She saw the loss of future generations as teachers attempted to brainwash students into reporting on any antirevolutionary activities committed by parents or siblings. She experienced the loss of community as neighbors spied on each other with a false sense of duty to the government over all else.

And yet, despite all the losses, my grandmother never lost hope.

But she knew that hope also required action. Hope was that flicker of light when you were sitting alone in a dark room. But when you added action to the mix, then you could use that light to get up and guide you to something new and wonderful.

When things in Cuba seemed the bleakest, when she believed that she could lose her children—physically and spiritually—my grandmother chose to act. She made the decision (along with the parents of more than fourteen thousand other Cuban children) to send her teenage daughter and young son to the United States, by themselves, through a secret mission called Operation Pedro Pan. At that moment, she did not know what would happen. She didn't know if, or when, she would be reunited with her kids. But she had hope . . . and a plan of action.

Months later, my grandmother was faced with another choice. A choice between her country and her children. To be with her kids and preserve the freedom they'd found in the United States, she had to give up her country. Leaving Cuba, never to return, was the only way to be a family again. And for her, family was everything.

Over the years that followed, my grandmother kept her happy, infectious attitude. Through all the hard times of starting over in a new country, she focused on the positives of being together and the opportunities offered to them. It was no surprise that she and my grandfather eventually chose to move from Miami to a small southern town just so they could be close to my sister and me. They moved to a place where they had no friends and no one outside my family understood them. But in the end, it didn't matter. My grandmother embraced it all. And through her actions (which included making delicious Cuban desserts, like flan or *natilla*, for the neighbors) she became everyone's *abuela*.

And so there we were at the church softball game, Abi grinning from ear to ear, shouting about pasta. She was beaming with pride, but I wanted to crawl under the bleachers and hide.

"Abi, no." I shook my head at her.

She seemed confused by my reaction.

A few people around her smiled and nodded. The crowd stood up and, as they shouted, "Let's win it!" she shouted "Linguine!" for the second time.

It was what she thought they were saying.

And to be honest, between the southern accent of the fans and my grandmother's Cuban accent, *linguine* and *let's win it* did sound very similar.

Abi looked at me with the kindest of eyes. In the end, she did speak the language of her American friends. They all understood something that I hadn't. A common thread didn't depend on having the same language, religion, race, or gender . . . It was something much greater. A belief in our neighbors, that we were all in this together, and that doing good things for each other made us all better.

In later years, this singular moment ended up helping me through the hard times of having to move away from that small town to the big city of Miami. I was almost fifteen and had to face the fact that for the first time in my life, I had no friends. I was the new kid with a southern accent going to a school that had more people than my hometown. I had never felt so alone.

But my grandmother's example continued to shine ahead of me like a beacon, reminding me that there was light at the end of the tunnel. I found power in the knowledge that if my grandmother could make strangers her friends, then maybe I could do it too. Eventually, just like my grandmother, my adopted city became home.

So in the end, perhaps it was fitting that although I always called my grandmother Abi, everyone else called her by her real name . . . Esperanza, the Spanish word for hope. Abi had always shown me love and kindness, but on that one particular summer evening, she taught me the importance of living in a nation of hope . . . even if it comes simply from believing in the power of baseball pasta.

HOPE NATION

DAVID LEVITHAN   LIBBA BRAY   ANGIE THOMAS
ALLY CONDIE   MARIE LU   JEFF ZENTNER
NICOLA YOON   KATE HART   GAYLE FORMAN
CHRISTINA DIAZ GONZALEZ   **ATIA ABAWI**
ALEX LONDON   HOWARD BRYANT   ALLY CARTER
ROMINA GARBER   RENÉE AHDIEH   AISHA SAEED
JENNY TORRES SANCHEZ   NIC STONE
JULIE MURPHY   I. W. GREGORIO   JAMES DASHNER
JASON REYNOLDS   BRENDAN KIELY

ATIA ABAWI

*Don't Listen to the A**holes*

IT WAS ONE OF MY last days of twelfth grade. The spring roses were in bloom, and I was high on life. High school was coming to an end, and the transition into the new, exciting journey of university life was about to begin. I was becoming an adult. Ready to start on a path that would lead to an unknown future with the pursuit of my admittedly far-fetched dreams. Going away to college was also going to give me a freedom I longed for after growing up in a household that was fairly strict, compared with those of my friends. This was going to be a journey into a new world, and I couldn't wait to see what lay ahead.

Nothing could get in the way of my happiness, or so I naively thought.

I had already been accepted into the university I wanted to attend and had picked my major, whereas most of my friends were still undecided. Like most high school seniors who had received their college acceptance letters and begun the enrollment process, I let my schoolwork slide and gave priority to my social time. My last hurrah with my high school friends.

I wasn't suffering from the stress of trying to decide what I wanted to study. I knew from a very young age I wanted to be a journalist. When I was seven, I even had a small notebook in which I would tape my classmates' school pictures and write short news stories of the famous people they would become. The kids loved it as much as I did, and gave me more pictures to write more stories.

Another driving force for my journalistic dream inadvertently came from home. I had grown up watching television network news every day. This was before cable news became a thing—cable was more of a luxury back then. We'd flip back and forth between the major networks' nightly news programs in the hope of catching a glimpse of my parents' homeland, which was falling apart. As much as they focused on shielding their children from the real world, they couldn't, not really. Our mere existence made it difficult to do so. We were refugees of war. That meant my parents' comfortable, happy lives had been ripped away from them in an instant and their existence had become that of pure survival—not so much for themselves as for their children.

My family was originally from Afghanistan. My parents grew up in the bustling capital city of what was then a very peaceful country. They were always surrounded by family, love, and comfort. But all that changed in 1979, when the Soviet Union gained a foothold in the land and a deadly war began. The Communist parties took over and began their massacres that would last for a decade—the first of several gruesome wars that continue to devastate the country. It was 1981 when my parents were forced to leave. My brother was only two years old, and my mother was eight months pregnant with me. I was born in Germany, where we first arrived as political refugees, and was a year old when we were welcomed into the United States to begin our new lives.

Assimilating into American life wasn't always easy. But we were always grateful to a nation that allowed us to come in and start fresh while our Afghan countrymen continued to be slaughtered for thinking the wrong way and having the wrong last names and wrong political beliefs. Unlike many countries, the United States gave everyone the chance to work hard and achieve success. Some had to work harder than others, but the opportunities were there. We faced a lot of challenges and bumps along the way. Some roads even seemed blocked at times, but there was always another path to take. And if I learned anything from my parents, it was that with hard work, the impossible becomes possible.

But I digress. Back to my senior year.

I had already experienced having teachers who disliked me merely because of my religion and race, which I always found confusing, because I was raised not to judge or hate, and to believe that our educators were above such ignorant convictions. There was the chemistry teacher who found out about my Afghan heritage, toward which she had a deep-seated hatred because of her own racial background—a feudal history I wasn't even aware of, because I grew up in northern Virginia and not the Central and South Asia of sixty years earlier. There was also my US government teacher who hated Muslims, as evidenced by her snide and humiliating comments toward certain students, including me. And there were others who associated skin color with laziness and unworthiness, and students who were not worthy of their time. It was quite blatant at times.

Although I had encountered a few of those bad apples, I thought

Mr. W was unlike them. He wasn't the most encouraging or the friendliest teacher I had had, but he was young and fresh and never really showed disdain toward me—at least I never interpreted it that way. I knew he was quieter around those of us who weren't his obvious favorites. But I was okay with that. I had no desire to be a "favorite." I just wanted to be graded and assessed for the work that I put in. I was by no means a perfect student, but I did pretty well grade-wise and tried to be as respectful as possible to those around me, especially faculty.

On the final day of our Advanced Placement Journalism course, Mr. W rolled in a metal cart carrying a giant box TV and VCR. It was a sight that brought pure joy at the end of the school year—and a sign that the teachers were slacking off too. He said he wanted to talk about our future and how journalism would be a part of it before he popped the great American classic *Citizen Kane* into the VCR and then flicked off the lights.

One by one Mr. W called my classmates by name, and each quietly walked to take the seat across from his desk. As I watched the movie, I peeked at the smiling faces of students sitting back down at their own seats after what I could only imagine was encouragement from Mr. W about their bright futures. My friend Alyssa bounced back to our table beaming. She was the type of person who had a smile that could brighten up a room, even more so after receiving good news.

That's when I heard my name.

I still remember the nerves and excitement that permeated my body. I had always been apprehensive and nervous about sharing my dreams with anyone—afraid they would laugh in my face. Or that they'd have the same thoughts that played in my own head. *You're not pretty enough to be on TV. You're not smart enough to report on such serious stories. You're only a female. No one wants to hear the news from an "ethnic" girl.* But I'd been a student of Mr. W's for three years by then—starting with Journalism I, then Photojournalism (Yearbook), and now Advanced Placement Journalism. I received decent grades in all his courses—mostly As and Bs. And if he didn't think I was good enough, it surely would have been expressed in my scores or in his treatment of me.

So I decided he would be the first person outside my family with whom I shared my dreams. I figured he of all people would get it. And from all the smiles I saw around me, I knew he would encourage me. He was a professional; he was an educator of young minds. This was my moment to be vulnerable, because I was safe from rejection and ridicule. We were seniors about to head into our adult lives. If teachers didn't encourage our dreams—who would?

I sat in the seat in front of him, and he stared at me, inexpressive and serious. Mr. W was the type of man who could witness a litter of puppies rolling around in a box and keep a straight face while saying how majestic it was.

"So, what is it that you want to do with journalism in the future?" he asked.

"Well," I said, smiling, thrilled to finally have the courage to share my dream out loud, "I want to be a foreign television correspondent and maybe an anchor. I want to go out and see the stories myself and report on them for TV. I want—"

"I'm going to stop you right there," he cut me off. "You're never going to make it. You don't have it in you. Don't even bother wasting your time." His deadpan eyes now seared into mine. In hindsight, I realize his lack of communication and his inexpressiveness may have been limited to students like myself, the ones he didn't believe in. Looking back, I see that he did go out of his way to ask his "favorites" to work on the school newspaper or work on special assignments—but that had never been directed toward me.

I just froze, puzzled. It took a second before his words really registered, making my stomach drop and instantly shattering all the dreams I had built since I was a young girl. The silence was deafening as his unblinking brown eyes cued me to get up and walk away. He sat there unbothered as my own eyes dropped, taking with them any confidence I had left in my already insecure teenage soul.

I instantly felt like a vulnerable little girl again, no longer a young woman on the verge of adulthood. Even now, decades later, I picture a seven-year-old with pigtails walking back to her seat—not a seventeen-year-old.

So many thoughts scattered through my mind in that short walk back to my seat. *How do I change my major? Everyone says it's impossible to do so after you've declared it. Oh God, what should I study now? I was a fool to think I had a chance. Is he laughing in his head at how ridiculous I am?*

As I sat back down, Alyssa grinned at me, giving me a thumbs-up. All I could do was feign a smile back, pretending it had all gone fine. I didn't want to go through the humiliation of telling someone else my foolish dream. If Mr. W, the head of the number one school newspaper in America, said I wasn't good enough, then I knew too that I wasn't good enough.

Let me just remind you here that I grew up in a first-generation Afghan American family. My parents gave up everything they'd ever known for their children. They worked diligently in their new American lives, breaking their backs to ensure their children's future. Their aspirations for my brother and me were for us to become either a doctor or a lawyer—in that order. Dreams were a luxury in a world where your life could be torn away from you in a second. What one needed in this world was stability with a steady foundation, not frivolous goals. And after years of telling me to give up on the silly idea of becoming a journalist, they were suddenly, and reluctantly, on board, and I didn't have the heart (or maybe it was pride) to tell them that I finally agreed with them.

The good news, although it didn't feel that way at the time, was that it was difficult to change your major on such short notice. I also didn't want to become an "undecided" as I went into my first year of college. So I started at Virginia Tech that following autumn and was assigned classes that coincided with my communications major. And despite having an adviser in my department telling me that I was a perfect candidate to be a television journalist, I didn't believe him—his pervy nature didn't help in making me trust him. I added electives that I thought would work for a more practical minor, which I could eventually change into a double major. I tried marketing, psychology, sociology, and economics before finally settling on international studies—which contained the only other classes that I found as interesting as my communications courses. At Virginia Tech I had instructors and professors who helped me recapture my interest in journalism. Two who really stick out to this day were Professors Dale Jenkins and Sam Riley. Professor

Jenkins reinvigorated my interest in public speaking, and Professor Riley reminded me how versatile journalism could be—they made class compelling by allowing us to express ourselves and stories in unique and often fun ways. They never picked favorites, and even when you started slacking, they would find ways to reenergize and encourage each and every student. Their passion was infectious. I will always be grateful to these two men for reigniting my love for the industry.

It was at Virginia Tech where I was introduced to TV production. And during my junior year I decided to volunteer at Virginia Tech Television (VTTV). I didn't take it as seriously as my student colleagues who had no doubt that their futures would be in television. In a way, I envied their confidence. Despite continuing with my journalism curriculum, deep down I felt it was something I would have to give up soon enough. Mr. W's words continued to creep into the back of my mind whenever I even toyed with the idea of pursuing reporting.

There was a problem, though. As the years progressed, so did my parents' support for following through with my dream. My mother took particular interest and had me tape my VTTV clips and bring them home with me whenever I visited them for the holidays or a weekend. She would watch, smiling, and kiss me with pride—no matter how much I had stumbled on my words or gotten caught in a fit of giggles, forcing a commercial break.

One day she called to tell me she had bumped into a woman in the fitting room of a clothing store in our area. My mother told me that the woman had approached her, asking what she thought of an outfit she was trying on. As they started to chat, my mother told this woman that she looked very familiar. The woman then introduced herself as Hillary Howard from the local CBS News station. My mother went on to tell her about me and my studies. That's when my mom's new acquaintance handed her a business card and told her to have me get in touch for a tour of the station.

It was my senior year of college by then, and other events in my life had also contributed to my turning into an introvert and losing more confidence. I didn't want to contact Ms. Howard—I was too nervous. I didn't want someone in her position to laugh at me or ridicule me. I wasn't in the mood for more rejection and feeling smaller. But my mother, being my mother, badgered me until I finally emailed her.

When I arrived at the WUSA studios one very cold and snowy winter morning, I was greeted by a smiling and kind Hillary Howard. She was the type of person who instantly made you feel at ease and comfortable in an environment that was far from the everyday norm. And a TV studio like that one, for most people, was not normal. She introduced me to both on-air and off-air colleagues, the majority of whom were just as welcoming. One was a naysayer, but he was easy to ignore among the encouragement. It was exciting to witness the adrenaline and dynamics that went into the morning newscast, and by the end of the visit I knew this was something I wanted to do. I had been bitten by the bug, some would say. As she was dropping me off to exit the building, I built up the courage to ask Hillary if she was willing to mentor me. With pure honesty and kindness she told me that she wouldn't be the best mentor but knew who would be, and she jotted down the contact information of a former colleague at the local Fox affiliate.

And she was right: John Henrehan was the best mentor a cub reporter could ask for. He taught me television journalism in a way that you could never learn in school. He introduced me to two local cable stations that had daily thirty-minute newscasts and told me to go volunteer, to live the news so I could learn the news. John taught me that the best way to master news writing wasn't from reading books, or listening to my professors, or even from him— he told me that the only way to learn was to write the stories and keep writing them. My first story could take days to finish, he told me, but by my fortieth I should be able to pop out a news story in minutes—and I did. He reminded me that becoming a journalist requires hard work, patience, and humility.

At one of the stations he introduced me to, I learned quickly about the real-world vultures who try to tear you down. That's not just something that stays in high school; it follows you all through-out life. At that particular station the news director harassed and bothered anyone he thought would get in the way of his success, and in his mind that was everyone. But at the other station, I was introduced into a journalistic family, the CTV76 family, who were welcoming and encouraging. I still hold all of them dear to my heart today. At CTV76, the team helped me improve my skills every single day I was with them. My success was their success.

But I still wanted something different from the daily grind.

As I graduated from local news in Maryland, I was hired as an entry-level journalist at CNN. I went from reporting on real news stories at my local cable station to printing out scripts for news directors and anchors who didn't know my name—or care to learn it. I wasn't just at the bottom of the ladder, I was the dirt beneath it, so I knew it was time to climb. I volunteered in the various news departments on my days off, hoping hard work would pay off. At CNN, I discovered that bullies and vultures exist even at the shiniest of networks (because of ageism, sexism, racism, or their own demons), but they had mentors within their doors too, similar to Mr. Henrehan, who went out of their way to help you.

Jealousy is rampant in all walks of life, especially in the field of journalism. Every step up you take, someone is grabbing at your feet from below to pull you back, and there are those above you who are trying to push you down and kick you off the ladder. What I learned is that you have to look for those hands that are reaching below to help you climb up and those underneath that are encouraging your flight—and often you are the one who needs to be vocal in asking for their assistance. You also need persistence and belief—especially when times get tough. There were many occasions when I wanted to give up and started to think that maybe that journalism teacher and the bullies along the way were right. What kept me on track was realizing that there comes a point when your dreams are no longer just yours; they also belong to those who encouraged you all along.

Following your passion is not an easy task. Little in life is a breeze. But it does feel damn good when you defeat the odds. The harder the challenge you overcome in life, the stronger you become as a person.

Despite the discouragement I met along the way, I went on to become that foreign correspondent I had dreamed of becoming. I covered both the Afghanistan and Iraq wars. I sneaked into Myanmar while the military junta was hunting down journalists.

I moved on to NBC News and covered the British royal wedding between Kate and Wills and then the death of Osama bin Laden in Pakistan. I met many amazing people from all over the world and felt honored to have been used as a vessel to share such important stories of everyday people as well as dignitaries. I'm no Barbara Walters or Diane Sawyer, but I accomplished what I wanted to, and it definitely had its ups and downs along the way.

Many friends with whom I shared my high school journalism class story throughout the years asked if I would confront my former teacher. My answer was always no. The older I grew and the more bullies I met, the more I realized that I wasn't the problem, they were. Trying to stop someone from accomplishing their dreams or finding happiness in someone's failures comes from darkness in the heart—whether that be a stain of jealousy, envy, or something else. That gloom eventually consumes the person that holds on to it. And despite their achievements, they never find contentment or happiness. This is not just something I think; it is something I've seen time and again. And when you are that helping hand for someone else's dreams, there is no greater joy than watching their success—something the darker of hearts won't ever come to know or feel.

But I did meet Mr. W again.

In the summer of 2015, I was invited by the US State Department to speak about my first young-adult novel, *The Secret Sky*. The book was based on the experiences I'd gained as a journalist in Afghanistan and was written in hopes that readers would understand the culture and situation of the complex country in a deeper way than they would from just a short news clip and report. I had posted the flier about the talk to my Facebook page and told friends and family in the area to attend if they could.

I arrived at the Harry S. Truman Building in Washington, DC, on a hot and humid July day with my six-month-old son and mother-in-law. We waited in the building's main lobby and watched as friends and former colleagues from around the world checked in to watch me speak. The excitement was building to share my experiences and the new book. A high school friend I hadn't seen since she used to drive me to school in the mornings approached us. I was thrilled to see a face from my high school days.

As we were catching up, she dropped the bomb. "Guess who's coming?" she asked.

"Who?" I responded.

"W," she added excitedly, waiting for me to reciprocate her enthusiasm.

"Oh." I gazed at her, trying to remember if through our sporadic Facebook messages over the years I had told her about his crushing words. I was more than sure I had. But maybe she had forgotten. In the end, she was one of the students he adored, and in return, she held him in high esteem. The thrill on her face began to fade when she saw the lack of it in mine.

When Mr. W walked through the building's shiny glass doors, he approached me and said hello. I uncomfortably greeted him back.

After he signed in and received a visitor's badge, the awkwardness continued. I had nothing I wanted to say to him, feeling caught off guard. So I just asked how he was doing as we were all escorted toward the elevators.

I really didn't know how to fill the moments of uncomfortable silence, so I asked another mundane question. "How is Annandale High School?" I had always been proud to be a part of Annandale because of its mass diversity. When I attended, the walls of our school held students who came from 129 different countries and spoke seventy-four languages. As First Ladies, Hillary Clinton and Michelle Obama had both visited the school because of its great diversity.

Mr. W's response felt like a slap to that beauty. "Filled with Hispanics and no more white people," he said, unashamed. My former high school friend whacked his arm, signaling him to quiet down so others wouldn't hear his remark.

Shocked and disgusted, I didn't know what to do or say. Around me were friends and colleagues from all over the world, and others whom I didn't know. I knew I didn't want to cause a scene. I decided the best thing to do was walk away from this poisonous person. I had already said goodbye to his toxicity long before, and I didn't want to be around it for one second more. Too much good had come from the kind people I had met along the way, and leaving behind the bad had led me to a fairly content life.

So as I spoke at the podium in the library of that government building, I focused on the faces in the room I had met along the way as my dreams were coming true—the embassy officials, the friends, and the colleagues I had met through the years. They were black, white, and everything in between. All of them had defeated their own bullies and demons to get to where they were.

Many people were upset with me for not confronting Mr. W that day. For not reminding him of what he had said to me so many years earlier. But I acted the way I was raised to. I try my best to show kindness and courtesy even to those I may feel do not always deserve it. But I do regret one thing about that last meeting with Mr. W: it is that I didn't confront him about his words in the here and now. I let keeping civil hold me back from telling him that his words were wrong and uncalled for. As a journalist I had always been taught to be objective and listen, including to those you don't necessarily agree with. But I have learned in the last year, more than ever before, that sometimes we have to be loud.

In life, we will always feel like we don't belong. Even those who look comfortable in life have their challenges and insecurities. Those bullies, I've learned, are the least confident of all. They're just paper tigers. We will always find people who criticize us. Some of that will be constructive, so I listen. Other times it will be hurtful. I've learned to not take it personally, because it is a reflection of those people's own misgivings. But even with age and experience, it can be difficult.

I had a young relative tell me she had Mr. W as her teacher at AHS in recent years. One day, after he had bragged to his class about having had a student who went on to work at CNN and NBC News, she approached him and told him she knew what he had said to me all those years ago. His response to her was "Well, then, I guess she has me to thank for her motivation to succeed." But I am not grateful to him, nor am I ungrateful. All I know is that any success I may have had and, ideally, will continue to have is credited to those who encouraged and helped me: my parents, Professor Jenkins, Professor Riley, Hillary Howard, John Henrehan, my CTV76 family, and all those people I worked with who held their hand out for me along the way.

There will always be the naysayers and the roadblocks. Sometimes the person who was putting me down the most was myself. But no matter how challenging life became, I had to learn to believe in myself—and sometimes that meant listening to the encouraging words around me. In the end, your thoughts are all that really matter.

I once asked Helen Thomas, the renowned journalist and one of my journalistic heroes, her secret for accomplishing one's dreams, and her answer was plain and simple: "This will sound cliché, but never give up." She was right.

HOPE NATION

DAVID LEVITHAN   LIBBA BRAY   ANGIE THOMAS

ALLY CONDIE   MARIE LU   JEFF ZENTNER

NICOLA YOON   KATE HART   GAYLE FORMAN

CHRISTINA DIAZ GONZALEZ   ATIA ABAWI

ALEX LONDON   HOWARD BRYANT   ALLY CARTER

ROMINA GARBER   RENÉE AHDIEH   AISHA SAEED

JENNY TORRES SANCHEZ   NIC STONE

JULIE MURPHY   I. W. GREGORIO   JAMES DASHNER

JASON REYNOLDS   BRENDAN KIELY

ALEX LONDON

Different Dances

I TOOK MY BEST FRIEND'S girlfriend to junior prom, so you could call this a prom story if you wanted. Although there isn't much romance, this is a kind of love story. There isn't any kissing, but there is some violence. Also: drag.

The story starts during a class I wasn't in with a girl I didn't know and her boyfriend whom I didn't know either. The class was a US history elective at the all-girls prep school across the street from the all-boys prep school where I went. Juniors and seniors could take classes at either school, so our experience became coeducational toward the end, after years of single-sex isolation during which gender roles were strictly established and rigidly enforced.

The boys wore ties and played sports. The girls wore skirts and took home ec. They also played sports, but the boys did not also get to take home ec, which struck me as a kind of injustice. My terrible lacrosse playing has not come in handy in adult life, and I still don't know how to sew on a button. At my school, anything too far from preppy made you a "freak," anything even slightly feminine made you a "fag," and anything at all creative made you an "art fag." Most boys never strayed from the gender norms, even in the classes they took.

My best friend, Ryan, was not most boys.

The US history elective at the all-girls prep school was called the Devil in the Shape of a Woman and covered the history of witchcraft in America from a feminist perspective. There were only two boys in that class and one of them was Ryan. He was the only junior.

Sitting in class one day as they discussed accusations of witchcraft as the violent policing of coercive gender constructs, a senior named L—— mentioned her plan to go to prom in a tuxedo, while her boyfriend would wear a dress, because "screw meaningless gender signifiers and screw the conservative school cultures that enforce them. Deconstruct the gender binary!"

Ryan overheard the plan and told L—— that it was pretty rad or cool or totally cowabunga, dude, or however we talked back then. The slang is lost to history; the sentiment is not. Ryan loved anything that would stick it to The Man or, as he now describes it, "undermine the social rigidity of our school's oppressive gendered culture."

At the time he probably just said, "Fuck yeah!"

That could've been the end of the story and I never would have known or gotten involved or nearly had a panic attack on the dance floor at junior prom had L——'s boyfriend not chickened out. He didn't wear a dress. He didn't even wear an interesting tuxedo. He wore a black rented tux like almost everyone else at the dance (except for some of the lacrosse players, who went with the tuxedo jacket and pastel shorts look). L—— wore a dress, and their prom unfolded like every other prom at our school ever had since its founding in 1897. This, by the way, was all happening during the school's centennial year, 1997.

I'm not sure the hundred-year anniversary of institutional gender policing at prep school passed through Ryan's mind, but he definitely felt like L———'s plan shouldn't be abandoned because her boyfriend was too insecure. He offered to take her to junior prom and promised her he would wear the dress this time and she could wear the tux and they could still say screw you to the meaningless gender signifiers and screw you to the conservative school cultures that enforced them, just for a slightly younger crowd.

She said rad or cool or totally cowabunga, dude, or whatever, and the plan was set in motion.

The only problem was that Ryan had just started dating E——— and she wanted to go to junior prom with her boyfriend, not an unreasonable request if you liked the ritual of the school dance with its formal attire and corsages and clusters of hormonal teenagers gawking at each other across the dance floor.

I did not.

I was not a school dance sort of guy. I was too self-conscious to like dancing in public, and I definitely did not want anything to do with school-sponsored events filled with most of my classmates. Some of my classmates might have been good guys—some of them turned out to be—but at the time, *all* of them terrified me. I had only two close friends, Ryan and a metalhead hockey player, T———, and in a way they both terrified me too.

I didn't want anyone to know me too well, not the real me anyway. None of them knew I was gay—no one did—and I worked very hard to keep it that way. I tried not to do anything that crossed the unwritten Rules for Boys that would've given me away. Even though I liked the theater kids, I didn't dare get too close to them, in case that made my queerness more noticeable. I avoided playing sports, because exposing how bad I was at them *would* make my queerness more noticeable. And when it came to girls, I veered madly from wanting to be seen with all sorts of girls—as cover—to keeping my distance in case it became too obvious to anyone paying attention that I was not like the other guys who flirted with them. In short, I organized a lot of my life and mental energy on keeping something invisible invisible. I didn't simply want to stay in the closet. I didn't want anyone to even suspect there was a closet in the first place.

So when Ryan asked if I would take his new girlfriend, E——, to the prom in his place, my brain did some Cirque du Soleil–level contortions.

On the one hand, I thought, going to the dance with an inarguably hot girl would be an excellent smokescreen.

On the other hand, going with my best friend's girlfriend would raise some eyebrows. Why didn't I go with a girl of my own? Why'd Ryan let me take his girlfriend? How'd he know I wouldn't make a move on her?

And then there was the question of why Ryan had assumed I didn't have a date already myself. Of course he knew I didn't, but how did he know I *wouldn't*? Did he suspect something? And why'd he want to wear a dress so badly anyway? Was he mocking me? Was he coming out to me?

All these thoughts raced through my head in half a heartbeat. The calculus of the closet is as quick as it is complicated. It's also totally self-centered. His wearing a dress to the dance had nothing to do with me.

And I genuinely liked E—— and didn't want her to miss the dance.

"Sure," I told Ryan. "I'll take her."

And the deal was done. She knew who her boyfriend was, and however weird she thought his junior prom drag plan was, she kept it to herself and agreed to go with me as her boyfriend's proxy. I did the whole thing. I wore an old tuxedo I'd gotten at a thrift shop. (It was plaid; my terrible fashion sense, although not deliberate, was definitely helpful in throwing everyone off the trail. Gay guys were supposed to dress well, right? I knew all the stereotypes and feared living up to any of them.) I got E—— a corsage; she got me a boutonniere.

Ryan arrived with L—— in her car. He'd paid for her tuxedo rental, an odd deference to gender formality. Black tie, black cummerbund. The rental place had to do some alterations because they didn't have tuxes cut for women, but the overall effect when she came into the converted gym was striking. Hair pulled back, a jawline that could cut diamond. She looked like a gender-bending James Bond.

But all eyes went to Ryan.

L—— had made his dress from scratch, and looking back, I can say with certainty that he was the only person at the junior prom in a bespoke outfit, but that wasn't why everyone was looking at it.

The dress was a blue-and-white floral-print maxi dress; its delicate shoulder straps amplified his bony collarbone and thin neck, flowed over his narrow hips, and revealed his armpit hair when he strolled through the gym. The music hadn't stopped and the gym's air was surely cloying, but I remember an airless silence. Someone near me muttered something about "art fags," and my heart double-timed its beat.

L—— and Ryan hit a spot on the dance floor, acting like they hadn't noticed all eyes on them but obviously reveling in the attention, and they danced. Desperate for the distraction, I danced with E——, glad my lack of rhythm wasn't at all the most remarkable thing happening at that moment. She gave a nervous laugh and rolled her eyes, but at Ryan or at me stepping on her foot I'll never know.

When the song was over, L—— excused herself to hang out with the other seniors who were there and whom none of us juniors knew. Ryan came over to us, cut in, and returned to his rightful place as E——'s date. I was a fifth wheel, happily enough, and we formed a little dancing and standing-around circle with T—— and his date. In a group, the dynamics were vague enough that I could disappear into them. We weren't two couples and a mysteriously dateless guy, just a shapeless gang of unpopular pals. But even in the group, I stayed aware, senses on high alert for every glance in our direction. I absorbed every muttered word about Ryan like it was a misplaced punch meant for me. The subtleties of gender and sexuality weren't a factor in the inner lives of my peers, and to them, cross-dressing meant gay, and gay meant weak, and weakness was to be pounced on, mocked, and eradicated. At least, that's what I feared and convinced myself was true.

Ryan was loving his role at the dance, dragging the lax bros and leaving the chaperones speechless. He wasn't really a guy who loved school dances either, but in political performance art he'd found his purpose. Drag is a fun-house mirror that amplifies identities, bends them, and mocks the absurdity of the costumes those of us who aren't in drag put on. It's a form of honesty.

We all put on drag, especially in high school: as students, as lax bros or math geeks or skaters or stoners or—like I did—as totally invisible normal straight teenagers without a weird thought or a forbidden desire in our hearts. The right shoes, the right brand shirt, the right slang—it was all a show we performed for each other and for ourselves, and in putting on that simple maxi dress, Ryan was showing all of us how silly our own drag performances were. It wasn't great drag; he'd made minimal effort at it—I don't even think he was wearing heels or makeup—but it forced everyone looking at him to reveal themselves and the drag *they* put on to fit in.

One guy in our class, S———, didn't like his junior prom being "mocked." His commitment to the gravity of school dances was a new thing, but he'd always been the sort of desperate alpha male whose machismo was so inflated, it could be popped with the pin from the flowers on the white floral boutonniere on his shoulder strap. The problem with guys whose masculinity can be threatened with an outfit is that they're not so great at self-control. Assuming everyone else is as fragile as they are, they think they can punch the world into becoming a safe space for their egos.

He made a move across the dance floor to tear Ryan's dress from his shoulders or to tear Ryan's head from his neck. It was unclear what the goal was, but two of his thick-necked friends restrained him. He was red-faced and huffing, like a cartoon bully, but he relented, although he hurled a few more "tranny," "loser," and "homos" our way before leaving us alone.

The last one stung. "Homos" was plural. How'd I get roped in to his insult? I was dressed in standard dude uniform. I'd gotten a haircut and had brought a girl to the dance. I didn't even jump up and down when the DJ played Madonna's "Like a Prayer." I'd done everything right!

I retreated deeper into the darkness of myself, put on the most "over-it" face I could, suggested prom was "so boring" and that we should just leave because it "sucked, like everything at this school." I wasn't about to let myself have fun or look like I was enjoying my best friend's drag act at all.

So it struck me as doubly dangerous when a slow song started and Ryan asked me to dance.

"It'll drive them crazy," he said, with a look over his shoulder to the other side of the room where S——— and the other goons were still sneering at us. Ryan had gotten into their heads, upset their sense of what their community of bros was and who was allowed in it, and now he wanted to take his performance to the next level. He had no idea what he was putting me through.

"Shall we dance?" He offered me his arm in gentlemanly fashion (his drag was inconsistent; the dress does not the drag queen make). If drag targets our absurdities, it's an imprecise missile. He'd hit a target he hadn't aimed at: me.

The hypersensitivity of the closet meant that I could see and hear S——— and the rest of them across the gym at the same time as I saw T——— and his date shaking their heads and laughing, and E——— trying to keep a good-natured smile on her face while also fighting the urge to grab Ryan and reel him in so they could just enjoy the dance as boyfriend and girlfriend. I have no idea. My fixation was on the boys and my fragile place in their ecosystem and my survival. I truly believed that if I was outed, I would die.

I took Ryan's arm anyway, because he was my friend and he was braver than me, and because part of me had a crush on him and because part of me was scared to say no and lose the only close friend I had. My entire identity was balanced on a razor's edge, and as my hands hit his hips and his hit mine and we began to awkwardly middle-school-style slow dance with two hundred sets of eyes on us, I realized three things at the same time.

The first was that it was actually kinda fun to dance badly in a place where everyone else preferred not to dance at all, and to ignore the sneers and the threats and the eye rolls and just do something silly with my friend. The unspoken but violently enforced rules about who got to dance with whom were joyless rules, and if I had to choose between the fake safety they offered and the joyful danger of supporting my boundary-pushing friend, I'd choose my friend every time. In spite of how much it scared me, I'd dance with him because that's what he needed me to do.

The second thing was that Ryan felt the exact same way. He didn't know the terror I was feeling or the earthquakes he'd triggered in my heart, but with all eyes on us and all the hate burning our way, I got a message he probably didn't mean to send: *Screw them—it's us against the world.* At that moment, there was nothing I felt I could've told him that would've pushed him away. Every joke we had that no one else understood, every oddball game we'd invented and absurd daydream we'd shared were the stitchings of a friendship that I couldn't possibly tear by simply being myself. It wasn't a romance, but if it wasn't love, then I don't know what is.

Third, I have never wanted a song to end sooner than Extreme's "More Than Words," but I still tear up whenever I hear it.

I didn't come out until almost a year later, but the process truly began that night, facing the straight-guy drag I put on every day and seeing it for the lie it was. I grew less and less afraid of the violence of my peers or the judgments of my community until the want of a real life overtook the fear of one. I came out in tandem with a boy I had a crush on, and suddenly, I had a boyfriend. We were, as far as we knew, the first open same-sex couple in the school's hundred-year history.

When my boyfriend, V———, and I considered going to prom, S——— was just as angry about it, just as threatening as he had been when Ryan wore that dress, but again some of his thick-necked friends told him to back off or told him it wasn't worth it. Some, surprisingly to me, told him he was being a homophobe. In the days leading up to prom, some of them even told me they had my back if it came to violence. I had more allies than I'd ever imagined. And Ryan, who'd never been in a fight in his life, was ready to fight for me too.

The year before, he'd tried to queer prom because he found the whole tradition completely ridiculous. One year later, he was ready to take a fist to the face for my right to be queer at it.

It wasn't easy being in the closet all those years, and it wasn't always easy after I came out, but if I could go back in time to talk to myself at that junior prom, when my best friend took me away from his girlfriend to dance, I'd want to say, "Enjoy it." Resisting the forces of closed-mindedness and hate is hard work and takes some risk, but it doesn't have to be joyless. Sometimes it's a march in the streets with banners and bandanas. Sometimes it wears a floral-printed maxi dress and sways to a mediocre pop song. Fear had gotten in the way of my joy for too long, and I decided never to let it do so again.

I ended up not going to senior prom, but not because of the threats. I wasn't trying to prove a point or to queer the institution or to mock its dumb gender conventions. I was just trying to be my actual self, as fully as I could, and my actual self didn't like school dances. I'd spent years trying to do what everyone else expected of me, and I was over it.

Instead, V—— and I put on tuxes and went to IHOP.

Ryan and his new girlfriend came with us before the dance—he wore a tux and she wore a dress—and then we split up. They went to prom, and we went out on our own and had a date as far from the school gym and the balloons and the DJ and the corsages and hormonal lax bros as we could get. I don't know how that night went for Ryan, but it was a memorable one for me and my first boyfriend. Our two bow ties didn't stay tied for long.

I didn't dance with Ryan again until sixteen years later, when my husband and I got married and he was in the wedding party. I don't recall the song, but all eyes were again on Ryan and me, and it turns out I didn't mind dancing with him so much after all. As teenagers, we'd danced in defiance. Now we danced in celebration, and I'm grateful he gave me the chance to do both.

DAVID LEVITHAN   LIBBA BRAY   ANGIE THOMAS
ALLY CONDIE   MARIE LU   JEFF ZENTNER
NICOLA YOON   KATE HART   GAYLE FORMAN
CHRISTINA DIAZ GONZALEZ   ATIA ABAWI
ALEX LONDON   **HOWARD BRYANT**   ALLY CARTER
ROMINA GARBER   RENÉE AHDIEH   AISHA SAEED
JENNY TORRES SANCHEZ   NIC STONE
JULIE MURPHY   I. W. GREGORIO   JAMES DASHNER
JASON REYNOLDS   BRENDAN KIELY

HOWARD BRYANT

The Dreadful Summer of 1991

WHEN YOU WANT TO BE a writer, especially for newspapers or magazines, you need experience. Being book smart is helpful, but there is no substitute for being in the field, covering events, learning the basics, actually talking to people. While most of my friends were having fun, sunning it up at the beach or backpacking across Europe, I spent my college summers looking for the internships I hoped would get me into the writing business.

My internship strategy was simple: Apply at the newspapers you respected the most, and if there were some you weren't familiar with, apply to papers in cool cities that intrigued you. That way, you'd either be at a paper where you wanted to work or in a city where you wanted to live. So began the 1991 summer job search—and I got neither.

I applied to the *Washington Post*.

Rejected.

I applied to the *San Francisco Examiner*.

Rejected.

I applied to the *Seattle Times*.

Rejected.

I applied to my hometown paper, the *Boston Globe*.

Rejected.

I got one call from a newspaper that summer, the *Lancaster Sunday News*, in Lancaster, Pennsylvania, sleepy farm town of the Amish and Mennonites and—did I mention?—lots of farmland. They called me in for a job interview, and it was a disaster. The editor, an old, balding white man with pinkish skin named Dave Hennigan, sat me in his office, looking at my young, black face with the high-top fade eighties style, and it clearly made an impression, because he asked me very few questions about my writing, my ambition, or my interests, but many—so many—questions about what it was like being black.

"How did your subjects react to you being black?"

"Do you think you could be effective not being in an 'urban' environment?"

"Have you ever not gotten a story due to white racism?"

I had interned before—at the *Philadelphia City Paper*, at the *Quincy Patriot Ledger* outside Boston, at *Philadelphia Magazine*, and at the *Philadelphia Inquirer*—and I had been the editor of my college paper at Temple University, and no one had ever asked me, essentially, whether being African American prevented me from doing my job. It felt like the kind of question someone would ask if they were looking for a reason not to hire you. Instead of saying what was in my head (*What kind of stupid question is that?*), I said the same thing, only nicer, more diplomatically.

"Sir, I'm here to do a job. And when you are sent out to get a story, you come back with a story. I don't think I would be much good to you or to myself if you sent me out for stories and I came back with excuses."

Dave Hennigan clasped his hands together, shook my hand and said thank you, and the bizarre interview was over. I went across the street to a restaurant, the Lancaster Dispensing Company, had lunch, and got ready to make the drive back to Philadelphia with one thought in mind: *Well, that was a disaster.*

Remarkably, I got the job.

Lancaster had three newspapers—the *New Era*, the *Intelligencer-Journal*, and my new paper, the *Sunday News*—all housed in one building. Of the three newspapers combined, there was one other African American reporter in the building, whom I never got to meet. The other black people were janitors or maintenance people. That was no big deal. I'd grown up in virtually all-white Boston and Plymouth, Massachusetts. I was used to being the only black person around.

But here, no one spoke to me. Nobody even *looked at me*. The editors gave me no assignments. Each day, I sat down and read the newspaper, ignored. When I would make eye contact with people in the hallway, they would look down. I wanted to get out in the field, write stories, talk to people, and learn how to be a reporter. People in the building treated me as if I were made out of Kryptonite. This went on for weeks.

I wanted out. Maybe the interview with Dave Hennigan wasn't so bizarre. Maybe he was trying to telegraph to me not to come here. If this was what being an intern was, what could the *real world* be like? I thought back to high school, where my guidance counselor in Plymouth told me that if I wanted to be successful as a black person, I had to leave Massachusetts because white companies wouldn't give you an opportunity to succeed. Even if they hired you, promotions would go to everyone but you. If you wanted to be successful, he said, you had to move to a place that was willing to give you a chance, and then once you proved yourself, Boston companies would not only recruit you, but be proud of you because you were from Boston. Being in Lancaster felt like the dead end my guidance counselor had described.

So, where would the hope come from? How could I survive this summer? What if this was what the white professional world was really like? Growing up around whites, I had already seen their underside, when your *friends* would try to explain their cultural dislikes of certain black people by saying, "I don't mind black people, but I hate niggers." They actually meant this as a compliment, that *you* weren't one of *them*—and I was supposed to be grateful they didn't see me as one of *them*. Whites would always remind you that you were the different one, like the time my friends and I went to go play hockey and one of the dads asked me if I was the puck. Get it? A hockey puck is black. I'm black. Hilarious.

William Raspberry was a columnist for the *Washington Post* at the time. My favorite columnist at my favorite newspaper. I noticed an article in the paper that said he had recently been in Lancaster and spoken at Franklin and Marshall College. So, desperate, ready to quit and return home embarrassed, I called him, a man I had never met or spoken to in my life. The day I called, I got lucky. He answered his phone.

"Do you understand why they treat you like this?" he asked. "It isn't really because you're black. It's because you're a threat to them."

"How can I be a threat? I'm just an intern. I'll be gone before September."

"Exactly. You'll be gone. You're a threat because you're young and talented and have your whole life of possibilities ahead of you. Most of those people there are stuck. They aren't going any farther than where they are right now. You'll be gone, to go see the world and dig into life and do all the things they'll never get to do."

We spoke for a few more minutes, and William Raspberry told me two things I would never forget:

"You also said you wanted to be a reporter, yes? Then why are you sitting around and waiting for them to tell you what to do? A reporter finds stories. Go to work. Dig into life. Learn about people. Don't just see the world, but feel it."

And . . .

"Just like in life, there are good people in that newsroom. Find the people who take an interest in your success. Spend time with them. Learn from them. And the people who aren't interested? Forget them. Only concentrate on the people who make you better, as a reporter and a person."

With a single phone call, the dreadful summer of 1991 turned. Gone was the wallowing and drinking coffee in my cubicle (I don't even *like* coffee!), replaced by the competitor I always believed I was (*Are you really going to let these people break you?*).

It was time for an attitude change. I didn't wait for the editors to speak to me. I pitched stories to them. Linda Eberle, the paper's graphic designer, was always friendly when I had to submit assignments, so I hung out in graphics a little more than in the cold newsroom. Linda taught me how to juggle (a skill I still have . . .). Slowly, the thaw began. Another reporter, Mark Beach, was huge into blues and jazz, and he started me on an appreciation of the music that has never left. And then there was the sports editor,

Bill Fisher, with whom I spent several lunches talking sports. Our conversations were so good, he told me they belonged in the paper, and I wrote an essay for him.

Most importantly, I went out and did the job, finding stories that were interesting but also sometimes hard. *Dig into life. Learn about people. Don't just see the world, but feel it* . . . I flooded my editors with ideas. It turned out that because Lancaster was between Philadelphia and Pittsburgh, an unusual amount of drugs were trafficked through this little, quiet town. As such, idyllic Lancaster County of trees and farmland had at that time the highest per capita rate of AIDS in Pennsylvania. I told my editors I wanted to write about it. They were reluctant because they did not want Lancaster reflected poorly, but ultimately I got to do the story.

I went to the local AIDS clinic and interviewed about a half dozen patients, all of them emaciated, unhealthy, and clearly aware that they would soon die. I was twenty-two years old. Many of them were not much older, yet from years of drug use and the effects of a deadly disease killing them every day, they looked much older.

Many of their stories were the same. They felt like outcasts. They felt like no one cared. They never believed there was hope for them. The word itself was so foreign, it was like it belonged to everyone *but* them. Some came from tough upbringings, but not all; others grew up rich. All ended up in the same place, convinced they would be dead within ten years—and all of them are almost certainly dead now. Most had a good sense of humor and even joked a little about what the diseases were doing to their bodies. As the patients told their stories, one said something that stayed with me. "Forget everything around me. I don't blame anyone else. If I had loved myself more, I would have never been in this position. I would have never been here. If only I had loved myself more."

If only I had loved myself more. How profound is that?

Later that summer, the Ku Klux Klan held a white supremacist rally in town. I asked to cover it, but my editors, fearing for my safety, wouldn't let me near the rally, and instead of the biggest story in town, I got sent to write about college moving-in day. For reals.

Certainly, there were people in the building who still treated me like Kryptonite. The editor, Dave Hennigan, never liked me, telling me when the summer ended that "there was more to the job than just giving a good interview." Ouch. Earlier, that might have hurt, but by the end of the summer I didn't care. People like him didn't matter anymore, and it wasn't because he was hard on me. I knew I had a lot of learning to do, and, news flash: The learning never stops.

Yet I had already learned about focusing on the work (after all, that was why I was there), the good people and the good stories about people, lost and maybe forgotten, stories that maybe hadn't been told before. Learning that I was maybe tougher than I thought and didn't quit carried far more lasting value than the odd judgment of a guy I'd never see again in my life. William Raspberry's inspirational words have always stayed with me. *Find the people who take an interest in your success. Spend time with them. Learn from them.*

And from that lesson came another: Help people. Whenever I need a reminder, I just think back to the dreadful summer of 1991 and how I felt when nobody was willing to help me—and how everything changed when somebody did.

DAVID LEVITHAN   LIBBA BRAY   ANGIE THOMAS

ALLY CONDIE   MARIE LU   JEFF ZENTNER

NICOLA YOON   KATE HART   GAYLE FORMAN

CHRISTINA DIAZ GONZALEZ   ATIA ABAWI

ALEX LONDON   HOWARD BRYANT   **ALLY CARTER**

ROMINA GARBER   RENÉE AHDIEH   AISHA SAEED

JENNY TORRES SANCHEZ   NIC STONE

JULIE MURPHY   I. W. GREGORIO   JAMES DASHNER

JASON REYNOLDS   BRENDAN KIELY

ALLY CARTER

The Two Types of Secrets

IN 2005 I BECAME A published author. That book, an adult work of "chick lit" called *Cheating at Solitaire*, isn't even in stores anymore. It sold approximately ten copies (most of them to my mom), so it wasn't exactly a huge professional success. But personally, it was a massive accomplishment, because it marked the moment when I became a published author—when I became the thing I'd wanted to be since I was twelve years old.

Ask any author what question they get asked most often, and the winner may very likely be "Did you always want to be a writer?" or "What made you decide to be a writer?" For me, the answer is pretty simple.

I grew up on a small farm outside a small town outside an even smaller, very rural community in Oklahoma. That's home—always has been. Always will be. The nearest big city was Tulsa, so when I was in middle school and started reading a book set in Tulsa, I thought it was pretty cool—I'd never read a book set in a place I'd actually been before. When my dad saw me reading that old paperback copy of *The Outsiders*, he told me, "You know she's from Tulsa, right?" and two things about that sentence totally blew my mind.

First, that the book wasn't just set in Tulsa—the author actually lived there. (*I could have seen S. E. Hinton at Walmart! At the mall! I could have eaten a corn dog beside S. E. Hinton at the Tulsa State Fair!*) This fact was simply amazing, because at that point in my life, I was pretty sure all books had been written by dead Europeans.

But the second part of that sentence was the one I was still thinking about days and even weeks later: She's from Tulsa. *She.*

In hindsight, twelve-year-old me must have been pretty sexist, because it had never even occurred to me that S. E. Hinton might be a woman. And when I learned that she'd actually written *The Outsiders* when she wasn't much older than I was . . . well, that was it. I was going to be an author. Why? Because that was something girls from Oklahoma could do.

So that was what I was *going* to do.

I just didn't tell anyone.

Ever.

I mean no one. Not my friends. Not my teachers. Not even my sister. I'm pretty sure my mom figured it out, because she was an English teacher and I kept asking her writing questions and asking to borrow her word processor (the old-school precursor to a laptop), but it was still something I didn't talk about.

Now I talk about writing all the time. "I'm a writer" is something I end up saying almost every time I meet someone new. Or fill out a form. I put it on my taxes, for crying out loud. (And there's nothing more official than taxes . . .) So I'm not exactly sure why *wanting* to be a writer was something I was so secretive about so early on.

Maybe I didn't need one more thing to make me stand out at school—one more reason for kids to label me a kiss-up or a snob because I needed to get good grades and all the teachers knew me because my mom worked just down the hall.

Maybe I didn't want any of the extremely hardworking grown-ups I knew to hear about this far-flung fantasy profession and tell me that writers don't make very much money (which most don't), or that there was no way I would ever meet someone who could help me get published (which I didn't). Or that it was time for me to grow up and get a practical dream—that my dream was silly or stupid or frivolous or one of a dozen other adjectives that kids, especially girls, are taught to fear at a very young age.

Maybe I didn't want someone to tell me not just that I *shouldn't* do it but that I *couldn't* do it. If someone had read one of my essays or looked at my grades or judged my work ethic and found me wanting . . . If just one person had told me that I didn't have what it took . . .

If those discouraging words had hit me at a bad moment during a bad day, that might have killed my dream right then and there. It might have killed it before it had really had a chance to begin.

I wasn't a published author yet and I was far from an expert on publishing, but I was the world's foremost authority on *me*, and I knew that about myself. I knew that I don't just take criticism—I take it to heart. And this dream was so tender and fragile and precious that it wouldn't have taken much to kill it.

So when I was twelve years old, I decided to become a writer.

And for probably a decade, I didn't tell a soul.

When I graduated from high school and left my small farm and small town and small community for a significantly larger university, I still kept my dream to myself. Sure, by that point, a friend or two might have figured it out, but my dream was still just that: a dream. Every semester my school would release a new schedule and I'd look longingly at the course catalogue, at the dozens of writing classes that I really wanted to take. But couldn't. Didn't.

Because even though my writing dream was still alive inside me, a part of me was still terrified of letting it out—of watching it die.

But the good news was that this was about the time I realized that you don't actually need a writing degree to do this for a living. You don't have to be a writing major to check out those textbooks from the library. You don't have to sign up for a program or get assignments from professors or belong to a club or a critique group.

If I wanted to be a writer, all I had to do was to write.

And there was no one who could stop me. Or judge me. Or tell me I was making a huge mistake.

So that's what I did. At night and on weekends. On my own and largely in secret. I was able to get a degree in agricultural economics, a very practical field, all while keeping my (seemingly impractical) dream safe and sound inside me, where no one could hurt it.

I did this through college.

I did this through graduate school.

I did this for years while working at my very practical day job (that I'd gotten thanks to my very practical degree).

I kept writing because, as the saying goes, that's what writers do. But it was more than that.

I kept writing because that was my dream, and dreams matter because of what you *do* about them—not because of what you *say* about them.

For more than a decade, I didn't talk about writing. I just wrote.

For more than a decade, this was my secret dream, and that made all the difference.

Another question that writers get all the time is "What do you do when you aren't writing? What do you do for fun?" Well, I, personally, love to cook. All kinds of things. I'll cook pretty much anything, but I've recently gotten into making homemade breads and hot rolls and pizza dough and all kinds of fun things that require yeast. Even though I've always loved to cook, it's taken me a while to work up the nerve to tackle these things, because yeast is really, really tricky.

Why? Well, you see, unlike most of the things in your pantry, yeast is *alive*. It might sit dormant in a package for months or years, but if you put it in some warm water—maybe feed it a little sugar or honey—it will activate. Pretty soon those little brown specks will start to grow and bubble, and if you do it just right, they can turn plain old flour into really yummy things. Which is awesome, but also terrifying. Because yeast is alive, which means it can also die. If the water is too hot, or you waited too long, or a whole host of other problems.

Hopes and dreams, I've decided, are a lot like yeast. They can sit dormant for a long time—years, maybe. Decades, even. And then with a little heat and a little nourishment, if you're lucky and smart and work with them just right, they might grow and expand and bubble—they might turn ordinary things into far better things.

I don't know what your thing is. Maybe, like me, it's writing. Or maybe it's science or math, music or dance. Maybe you dream of safer, happier communities or better schools or a world without bullies. Maybe your dream is one you can activate right now—start providing a little heat and a little food and a little time. Maybe this is your time to make something bubble up and grow.

But if it's not . . . If you're afraid that it might not be the right time for your dream and it might need to stay secret a little while longer, then that's okay too, because, like yeast, hopes and dreams can die along the way if we take them out under the wrong conditions or in the wrong environment or at the wrong time.

I think I knew that in middle school when I read *The Outsiders* and my dream was born. I think I knew that in college when I was taking agricultural economics classes during the day and writing up crazy stories at night. I knew it every time I scribbled frantically in a notebook and someone asked what I was working on and I said, "Nothing."

And I think a lot of you know it too.

For the last few weeks I've been taking writing questions from teens all over the world for a project that I'm working on. Some of the questions are what you'd expect. ("Did you always want to be a writer?" "Where do you get your ideas?" "How do you get your book published?") But I've been surprised by how many of the questions are about exactly this.

"What should I do if I show my writing to someone and they laugh at me?"

"Were your parents supportive of your writing, and what should I do if mine aren't?"

"When do you know if you should just give up?"

"I live in a really small town, and no one here can help me publish my novel. Should I even try?"

It's so incredibly easy for teens to feel powerless. Hopeless. Silly for dreaming of bigger or better or different. In many, many ways it probably always looks faster and easier and less scary just to do things the way they've always been done, to just follow the clear, obvious path.

Sometimes the only way to keep our hopes and dreams alive is to also keep them secret—dormant for just a little while. Sometimes the most powerful things we have are our secrets.

There's a line in my book *Don't Judge a Girl by Her Cover* that says that "there are two types of secrets: the kind you want to keep in, and the kind you don't dare to let out." This is by far the most-quoted line I've ever written. I see it on Twitter and Tumblr and Instagram all the time, and the more I think about it, the more it makes sense that this is the line that most resonates with readers.

For most of us, our hopes and dreams are that second type of secret. They take root inside us first, sometimes really deep down. And sometimes the scariest thing in the world is to let them out.

Sometimes—for some people—our secrets are the most powerful things we have.

Sometimes—for some hopes—we need times of quiet stillness for them to be cultivated and grow.

I don't know what your hope is or if you feel the need to keep it secret. Or why. But I do know that you are the world's foremost authority on you, and if keeping your dream secret—if keeping your dream private—is the best way to shelter and protect it and let it grow, then that's okay. And no one can take your dream away if you don't let them.

But remember: that doesn't mean now isn't the time to work, to prepare, to plan and collect the skills that you're going to need down the line. Because your time is coming. It's up to you to decide when to bring your dream out into the light, but it is also up to you to provide the heat and the nourishment. It's up for you to be ready.

There's a power in secrets. Secret identities. Secret missions. Secret dreams.

And no matter what your dream or your secret might be, I can't wait to see how it turns out.

HOPE NATION

DAVID LEVITHAN   LIBBA BRAY   ANGIE THOMAS
ALLY CONDIE   MARIE LU   JEFF ZENTNER
NICOLA YOON   KATE HART   GAYLE FORMAN
CHRISTINA DIAZ GONZALEZ   ATIA ABAWI
ALEX LONDON   HOWARD BRYANT   ALLY CARTER
ROMINA GARBER   RENÉE AHDIEH   AISHA SAEED
JENNY TORRES SANCHEZ   NIC STONE
JULIE MURPHY   I. W. GREGORIO   JAMES DASHNER
JASON REYNOLDS   BRENDAN KIELY

ROMINA GARBER

Born in Argentina, Made in America:
The Immigrant Identity

WHEN I WAS FIVE YEARS old, my parents uprooted our family from
Argentina to the United States.

I can still remember the terror I felt before my first day of kindergarten in Miami, Florida. My most pressing concern was how I
would tell my teacher when I needed to use the bathroom.

Yet the instant I walked inside the classroom, worry gave way to
awe: My classmates welcomed me into their world with shiny stickers,
colorful candies, and greeting cards, and everywhere I looked were
paper hearts and flowers and chocolates. I knew then my parents
were right: *This was the American dream.*

I came home that afternoon in a delighted daze, harboring my
delicious loot and gushing to my mom about how happy everyone
was to have me here—so happy, in fact, that they'd decided to throw
a huge party in my honor.

She didn't have the heart to tell me the truth.

It was February 14 . . . *Valentine's Day.*

On my second day of school, I was removed from regular classes
and placed in the English for Speakers of Other Languages program
so I could learn English. Until then, I'd been used to impressing the

grown-ups around me—my parents were always sharing anecdotes from when I was a year and a half because by then I could speak Spanish in full sentences—but in this new country, for the first time, I fell behind.

I rejoined my classmates when I was eight, but I had trouble reading, and I grew anxious anytime it was my turn to recite a passage in class. One day, my third-grade teacher, Ms. Balaban, noticed my struggle, and I've never forgotten what she did.

Everyone else was playing during recess, but she sat me down beside her and asked me to read a passage out loud. Whenever I stumbled on a word, she would cover it up with her ruler, revealing just one syllable at a time, until I managed to pronounce the whole thing.

It's the first "life lesson" I can remember learning, and I still apply it today. Anytime something feels overwhelming—whether it's my schedule or my workload or my feelings—I think of that ruler, and I try to break down whatever's bothering me into the smallest possible parts. Then I address each piece individually, without letting myself think of the larger whole.

If my third-grade teacher made me a reader, my fourth-grade teacher made me a writer.

Every day after lunch, Ms. Liotti would read to us from Shel Silverstein's masterpiece *Where the Sidewalk Ends*—and it was in those stories that I truly heard the English language for the first time.

I was nine years old when I discovered that nothing in this world could touch me as deeply as a well-placed word. I don't think I understood the meaning of Shel's poetry or prose—since I didn't hear conversational English at home, I still had a hard time following spoken language. Rather, what fascinated me was the way certain sentences sounded together, the way they could be arranged into symphonies, the way they awoke emotions in me that I couldn't rationalize.

I immediately began composing sentences of my own. I wrote my first poem—in Spanish—called "*Si yo fuera la luz*" ("If I Were the Light"), and I was shocked when my Spanish teacher liked it enough to submit it to the local county fair. But I was downright stunned when I won first place.

Soon I was carrying a Barbie binder with me everywhere, filled with my musings and poems and stories, written in both languages. I never shared them with anyone but Ms. Liotti.

In fifth grade, my parents took my sister and me on a trip to Boston, and I fell in love with the redbrick buildings of Harvard University. I was only ten, but as soon as we got back to Miami, I declared to my family that I'd made my choice of where I wanted to go to college.

Sixth grade was an election year, and my social studies teacher assigned our class an essay on the divisive issue of immigration. We were told to submit a page on whether we thought immigrants were a positive or negative influence on our country.

I ruled against them.

In my paper, I regurgitated everything I'd heard on TV: how immigrants were taking away our jobs and our opportunities and our safety. Pretty proud, I shared my finished essay with my mom that night. We read it together so that I could translate any words she didn't know.

I'll never forget the look she gave me when we finished reading.

There was so much pity in her expression . . . She must have seen in that instant that over a decade into my stay on this planet, I still had no idea who I was. Then she said, "*Romi . . . nosotros somos inmigrantes.*"

We're immigrants.

It was in that moment I realized that I'd been working so hard to memorize the English being spoken around me that I hadn't slowed down long enough to draw any connections. I guess it never occurred to me that I could be one of those people my new countrymen didn't want around.

But there was another, deeper realization that came with the label of *immigrant*: Even if I learned every word in the English dictionary, even if I made it to Harvard, even if one day I became a US citizen, I would never belong to this country. I would always be seen as an outsider who had come here to take away another's birthright.

If I made it to Harvard, I would be stealing an American-born teen's place. If I published a book in English, I would be using words that weren't rightfully mine.

And then came the most brutal revelation of all: Since I wasn't born here, I could never dream of running for president.

For the first time, my future, which I'd always seen as full of infinite possibilities, became finite. This may sound silly to some people, but for an ambitious person like me, it was a limitation on what I could become. A reminder to *know my place* in this country.

Even if I got my citizenship, I would forever be a second-class citizen. And all because of something completely out of my control: the part of this world I happened to pop out in.

Something changed in me then.

I began taking everything a little too seriously. I felt like I didn't have the luxury of being a kid, because I had to work harder to prove my worth and justify my place here.

When I was in seventh grade, my mom worried about how serious I was becoming, so she enrolled me in an acting class that my sister was taking. After my first lesson, my teacher made an offer to professionally represent me as my manager. I booked a handful of commercials that year, and then I spent spring break in Los Angeles with my mom, my teacher, and the other kids she managed for something called pilot season—the period when most TV shows get cast.

During the week I was in LA, I signed on with a movie agency, lined up a number of auditions, and had more fun than I'd had my whole life. When spring break ended, my manager invited me to stick out the full season, a couple of months—with a tutor, of course—to see what happened.

I said no.

I'd had perfect attendance for most of my education, and now that I was in middle school, our teachers stressed more than ever how important it was for college admissions that we not miss a single day of class. I didn't want to do anything that would put my chances of getting into Harvard at risk.

Maybe American kids could be movie stars, but I wasn't born here. I was an outsider, and if I wanted to earn my place, I couldn't make any mistakes.

Thus ended my brief acting career.

That was the first time I'd ever given up on something I

wanted—my first *sacrifice*. And the unexpected result was that I doubled down on my decision to go to Harvard.

Now that I'd made a sacrifice, there were *stakes* in place. If I didn't get in, I ran the risk of harboring some serious regrets—and that was a gamble I wasn't willing to make.

The rest of my school days were a blur of sacrifice. Studying came before everything and anything else. There got to be so many books in my house that my mom wouldn't give me any more allowance unless it was for food or clothes. So at fourteen, I began working an after-school job, and I didn't stop working until the week before I left for college.

I didn't have a boyfriend in high school until the end of senior year, once my future was secured. I remember a Friday evening my junior year when a persistent boy from my Spanish-for-Spanish-speakers class showed up to my house unannounced and told my mom he'd like to take me out, and she came to my room to beg me to go.

I said no.

I didn't expect her or my dad to understand my sacrifices because they'd grown up in Argentina, the country where they'd been born. They couldn't help me anticipate college requirements or fill out the right forms because they didn't know this new educational system. They didn't hear my teachers' warnings that things like too many absences or missed tests or Bs could be grounds for rejection.

Looking back, I wonder if it's because English is my second language that I've always taken its words so literally.

In eleventh grade, my family was finally approved for US

citizenship. We each had our own separate appointment to get sworn in, and mine happened to coincide with the timing of one of my Advanced Placement exams.

If there was one test I'd heard over and over and *over* again that we could not under any circumstances miss, it was an AP.

So when the day arrived, I went to school to take my test and blew off the INS.

The second the exam was over, the principal spoke over the intercom and called me down to his office.

When I walked inside, I was mortified to see my mom waiting for me and mystified to find her in a rage. *How could I miss that appointment? What was I thinking? Didn't I take our immigration status in this country seriously?*

But I did take it seriously. In fact, I took it so seriously that I didn't dare miss my unmissable test.

I looked to my principal, hoping he could explain the way things work to my mom, but he was staring at me with her same concerned expression. So I reminded him of how he and the other administrators warned us that we could not miss an AP test—it's administered only once, on the same date, nationally.

Then he said to me, as though it were the most obvious thing, "Well, of course there's a makeup day for extreme circumstances like these."

I was astounded.

At no point had any of my teachers mentioned a potential makeup day. At no point had any of my teachers mentioned that some absences were justifiable. At no point had anyone ever mentioned to me that I was allowed to prioritize *anything* over my schoolwork.

In twelfth grade, I got into Harvard.

And I felt like I could exhale for the first time since my immigration essay.

I'd done it. My sacrifices had paid off, and now nobody could claim I didn't deserve to be here, because I'd just proven my worth to the world.

As far as I know, only two members of my class of 800-plus students were accepted to Harvard—the salutatorian and me. When word spread that I was the second admission, I learned that my classmates had found a different justification for my achievement: They were whispering "affirmative action" behind my back.

The word I'd sacrificed so much to compensate for was still the only part of me people could see.

And in my moment of lucidity, I realized how foolish I'd been to ever let others determine my worth. No matter what I do, or how hard I try, my dual labels—"Argentine" and "American"—will always make me powerless to define myself, because people can assign me the identity that best suits their narrative at any given time.

I never should have accepted that I couldn't be president; I should have decided that I would be the one to change that law.

I never should have accepted that I could *either* be an actress or go to Harvard; I should have Natalie Portman-ed it and done both.

I never should have tried to fit into an existing and outdated system; I should have fought to modify that system to fit me and everyone else like me.

In today's America, we immigrants feel an even bigger push to justify our presence in this country. But just as it was with me growing up, this pressure isn't real; it's only perceived. It's just what some small-minded and misguided people want us to believe. People who are driven by their fear and not their faith. People who are afraid of the change we represent.

And these people know the only power strong enough to hold us back is our own.

We are so powerful. I'm a girl who had a hard time learning how to read who somehow wound up writing a best-selling book series in her second language and saw it translated into eight others. Imagine what more I could accomplish if I directed that power toward the world around me, toward those things I think I can't change.

Imagine what *you* can accomplish if you dare to believe in your own power.

Within each of us lies infinite potential.

Don't ever let a label take that away from you.

DAVID LEVITHAN   LIBBA BRAY   ANGIE THOMAS
ALLY CONDIE   MARIE LU   JEFF ZENTNER
NICOLA YOON   KATE HART   GAYLE FORMAN
CHRISTINA DIAZ GONZALEZ   ATIA ABAWI
ALEX LONDON   HOWARD BRYANT   ALLY CARTER
ROMINA GARBER   **RENÉE AHDIEH**   AISHA SAEED
JENNY TORRES SANCHEZ   NIC STONE
JULIE MURPHY   I. W. GREGORIO   JAMES DASHNER
JASON REYNOLDS   BRENDAN KIELY

RENÉE AHDIEH

Chah-Muh

I STRUGGLED A LOT WITH how to write this.

It seems simple enough to talk about oneself—one's likes, one's dislikes. One's dreams and aspirations. But whenever I'm faced with a situation in which I have to share a part of my past or a truth of my present, I find myself struggling for the right words. Perhaps this is why I tend to write fiction. It seems easier to share who I was and who I hope to be through the filter of characters, both large and small.

There are so many things I could talk about with respect to my identity and how it has shaped me. I'm not alone in this; everyone has memories from their pasts—epochs, if you will—that are bends in the road on their life's journey.

Identity is just one facet of it.

For me, it has become a huge part of how I perceive myself as a woman, as a writer, as a child of mixed race, as a wife, as a sister . . . I could go on forever. It's one of the first things I ask myself whenever I'm faced with difficult decisions.

Who are you? How does this choice shape who you are?

And who do you want to be?

When I was a child, I remember always wanting to be someone else. It carries over today. When I'm with my Korean family, I want to be more Korean. I want to know what they know, speak how they speak, and be comfortable as they are around each other.

It took years for me to realize that this will never happen.

I will never be Korean enough. I will never be American enough.

When I was twelve, I went to visit my mom's family in Seoul for an entire summer. I went with several goals in mind, many of them silly, some of which continue to make me smile to this day. I wanted to lose weight, because I was never thin enough, especially in Korea. My thighs were too thick, my backside was too round, my stomach was too soft; everything about me was "too" something. I laughed too loudly, ate too much, argued with my elders too frequently. So many things I wanted to change when I was twelve but wouldn't change now for all the world.

I also wanted to get new clothes. I know, I know. But I was twelve. Everything about being on the cusp of young adulthood is focused on the here and now. The immediacy of everything, especially emotions. I think that this is one of the reasons I so passionately love writing young-adult literature. Everything—a hand to hold, a look in the hallway, a pair of jeans with the tag still on them—everything has that delicious newness to it. A wonder I often think is all but impossible to achieve as an adult.

I wanted new eyeglasses too. Mine were horribly old and out of fashion. I'd chosen them when I was ten and thought purple was the be-all and end-all of colors. Tortoiseshell purple, at that.

My memories are also full of regrets.

Again, I know I'm not alone in this.

The next thing on my wish list was a new, Korean haircut. I'd sported long, unruly hair for most of sixth grade, and I wanted something fashion forward that would place me firmly among the ranks of stylish seventh graders at my new school.

Bear in mind, I was twelve. Sometimes I miss the time when those were the most important things to worry about.

Whenever we visited my mom's family, we would all share a room and sleep on the floor. Every morning, we would fold up our bed pallets and put them away in these huge, scented chests that left everything smelling like cedar, with a faint touch of my aunt's perfume. My brother, sister, and I would try to find American TV shows—often on the army network—to watch together. Or even simply try to find an American movie that wasn't hilariously dubbed. Family friends of ours had the *Anne of Green Gables* miniseries on VHS. I think we must have watched that at least ten times that one summer.

I think about this fact often.

I think about how we all could understand Korean television but still chose to watch something in English. Just as I think about how, when we were at home in America, my sister and I craved watching Korean dramas. Almost as though we were reaching across a void, trying to fill some unseen part of ourselves and make sense of our now—who we were and who we wanted to be.

I still remember what I was wearing the day we flew back from Korea. It was an outfit I had specifically planned, which I find comical, because a twenty-four-hour plane ride pretty much negates any attempt to look cute. There wasn't anyone I was specifically trying to impress. My dad was the one picking us up from the airport, and he would love me no matter what I looked like.

I picked that outfit for me. So I could come back home a new, better version of myself.

I'd also found a new pair of eyeglasses, which had been an amazing adventure all on its own. My second aunt had taken me to the underground market, a place that opens when the sun goes down and closes as its light peers over the horizon. Deep in this labyrinth of stalls and fluorescent lighting, she'd taken me to a small booth. In its center sat a wizened gentleman with stooping shoulders. She gave him my old purple tortoiseshell glasses—complete with a scratch through the right lens—and told him I needed a new pair. All he did was check the prescription. Then he told me to choose a set of frames.

I went with gold. Something that made me look older, wiser.

When he gave them to me, I felt like the sun's first rays peeking over the horizon.

I had my new outfit. My snazzy new haircut. My gold glasses.

Of course I hadn't lost weight. But we can't have everything.

Our flight into LAX from Seoul was horribly delayed because of some technical malfunction. When we deplaned, we were told we needed to go through customs, grab our bags, and have them rescanned and rechecked through security before we could proceed on our flight home to North Carolina.

Even though the woman at the gate assured us that our connecting flight would wait for us, my mom knew we weren't going to make it. She had the three of us throw our luggage onto two carts and haul ass through LAX. When we arrived at our gate, we were relieved to discover that our outbound plane was still on the tarmac.

It was clear our fellow passengers were not so relieved.

Their flight to North Carolina had been delayed, and they saw us as the reason why.

Our luggage had to be checked at the gate, which further delayed our flight. My mother's chest was heaving. We were all sweaty and tired. My brother had tripped during our run through the hell mouth that is LAX.

I still remember when I heard the first person say it.

"Do they not know how to check bags?"

It was a man probably around my dad's age.

As soon as he said it, a woman nearby said, "Of course they don't. They don't even know how to check their watch or show up on time."

Snickers followed.

A racial slur was thrown our way, meant to be under that man's breath, with the assumption that "they" wouldn't understand anyway.

I remember watching my mom close her eyes, tightly. This woman, who'd left her family and everything she knew at the age of twenty-four to study in America. Who'd bucked tradition and married a man from the West. Who had then gone further still and chosen to raise her children in a foreign country.

There's a word in Korean that I often have a hard time translating. Phonetically, it's pronounced "chah-muh." It's almost like the Korean version of "grin and bear it" or perhaps even "deal with it."

I stood and watched my mom "chah-muh" these people and their racist jokes.

In that moment, all the power and confidence I hoped my new hair, my new clothes, and my new glasses would grant me vanished like footprints along the shoreline.

Rage took hold of me. My fingers curled into fists.

I wanted to say something. I almost did. I wanted to let those hateful people know that this was not our fault. That we did indeed own watches. That we showed up on time. That we knew how to check our bags.

But mostly I wanted to tell them we weren't "they" or "those people."

I said nothing. It bothers me still that I said nothing. I wish this story had a better ending. The kind that inspires people to think outside themselves and their own identities and how they perceive other people in a moment.

The thing I took away most from this situation happened much later in my life. I'd always known that my mom left her family and everything she knew to come here. As a teenager, I often—cruelly—wished she had left more of herself behind. That way I could have my friends over and not have to ask her to speak in English around them, or worry that they might not like the "weird" food she served them for dinner. My desire to assimilate had long arms—arms that often reached outside myself and demanded that the rest of my family pretend to be people they were not.

All so I wouldn't be perceived as "other" or "those people." It was a selfish way to think and feel. Though I knew I wasn't alone in this—my younger brother and younger sister shared my fears—I missed out on many opportunities to light the path for them.

There were so many times I failed them. And failed myself at the same time.

Living in 45's America often makes me think of my story at the airport and the countless others I have from my lifetime. A lifetime of trying to be more American in North Carolina and trying to be more Korean in Seoul and failing horribly at both as I watch *Anne of Green Gables* on repeat.

There have been times when I've stood up and said something and times when I did as my mother did. "Chah-muh."

But these experiences have taught me an important lesson.

I am "they." I am "those people."

Because we are all Americans. We all came here with awkward stories. We all bore the wrinkles and scars of someone else's mistakes or situations over which we had no control. Maybe it didn't happen in my lifetime or yours. But it happened. And every person in this world has felt like they are too much of one thing and not enough of another in any given situation. My story is not unique, especially for a twelve-year-old. I only hope that—one day—I can convey to my own children how wonderful it is to live a life and tell a story unlike any other because it is theirs and theirs alone.

That they are beautiful for their struggles.

I never wore that outfit again. When I saw it, it brought back feelings of fury and inadequacy. Which was sad, because it really was cute. My haircut followed me through the first part of seventh grade. My glasses took me until I was fifteen and allowed to wear contacts.

This past year, someone tried to make my mom feel small and other because of a situation that was entirely not her fault.

I did not "chah-muh" that time.

And I will not "chah-muh" the next time either.

DAVID LEVITHAN LIBBA BRAY ANGIE THOMAS
ALLY CONDIE MARIE LU JEFF ZENTNER
NICOLA YOON KATE HART GAYLE FORMAN
CHRISTINA DIAZ GONZALEZ ATIA ABAWI
ALEX LONDON HOWARD BRYANT ALLY CARTER
ROMINA GARBER RENÉE AHDIEH **AISHA SAEED**
JENNY TORRES SANCHEZ NIC STONE
JULIE MURPHY I. W. GREGORIO JAMES DASHNER
JASON REYNOLDS BRENDAN KIELY

AISHA SAEED

The Only One I Can Apologize For

I AM CLUMSY. ASK ANYONE.

When I was six, I bumped into a pyramid construction of toilet paper at my local grocery store. (Turns out they are *not* the sturdiest of structures.) I was in a cast for six weeks because I tripped on carpet and tumbled onto my teacher. I've dropped pots, spilled tea, burned brownies by hitting Broil instead of Bake—you name it. As a result, I have probably said "I'm sorry" approximately 5,345,205 times (give or take a few). Not to brag, but I could probably teach college-level courses on the subject. And I know that although saying sorry is a valuable skill, not all sorrys are the same. Here are a few to avoid at all costs.

Sorry if I hurt your feelings.

Sorry, but you shouldn't be so sensitive.

As a general rule of thumb, if you're starting an apology with an *if* or a *but*, the best course of action is to take a deep breath and recalibrate, because an apology with qualifications is not a real apology and won't actually make the person apologized to feel any better or differently. In fact, those kinds of apologies have the tendency to make things *worse*. For an apology to be sincere and effective, it must come without reservations. No, it will not change what happened, but it tells the person you inconvenienced or hurt or harmed that you understand your actions were not okay. Here's an example of an apology without reservations, just off the top of my head:

I'm sorry.

See? It's not too hard. (And bonus points if you follow up and expand on how you feel and figure out how to make things right.)

Although I do believe being able to apologize sincerely and without reservation is an important quality to have, I admit I can go too far sometimes. I've apologized to the waiter when asking for a refill for my Diet Coke at a restaurant or for the check. I've said sorry to the doctor before I ask a question about my health. I've apologized for the thunderstorm when a friend has come into town to go river rafting. (Full disclosure: I *do* wish the power to control the climate was in my hands, but alas.) Apologizing can feel reflective if you do it enough, so it's important to remember that although apologizing for things that you actively did to harm, hurt, or inconvenience someone is a good trait, you should be sure to recognize when an apology is *not* in order. That is not as easy as it sounds.

I am an American Muslim. I know, that admission may feel like a random segue. It is not. Ask anyone who was out of diapers where they were when the attacks of September 11, 2001, happened and most people will remember. I know I do. I remember watching the footage on television and not understanding that what was playing was not the trailer to a movie but reality. I remember staring for a good five minutes as they replayed it, my mind unable to wrap itself around the magnitude of the horror.

I remember the next day. Plodding numbly down the hall at

the school where I taught second grade, during my lunch break. A colleague approached me. He pulled my hand into his. He said, "I just want you to know I don't blame you." Even now, I remember the confusion. Had my students started a food fight? Did someone stuff up the toilet? I went for my first instinct, to apologize, even though I had no idea what had happened. Then, he continued. "The twin towers falling—I spoke with my wife and we agreed, we're not mad at you."

The numbness I felt prickled into dread. A married couple, two teachers whom I had known all year, who smiled and chatted with me in the hallway as I discussed my new engagement and my wedding plans, had sat in their homes after the tragedy of 9/11 and discussed me and whether I was to blame for any of it. That they decided I did not have to shoulder the blame was beside the point; the fact that they had to consider it at all chilled me. I realized in that moment that my life as an American Muslim would be forever changed.

And it was.

I have stood next to my brother who was trying to make his flight back home to Miami only to discover he was put on a no-fly list because of his common name. I stood with my husband in an interrogation room at the airport when we returned from our honeymoon in Paris—he had a beard in his passport photograph and was therefore suspicious. (This is not a guess—we were informed that this was why we were held back for further questioning.) From the anonymous emails and comments in my inbox over the years to the vehicles that slowed down in front of my house until my father pasted a printed-out American flag on our window, everything changed after September 11. Although the married teachers had debated and discussed and ultimately chosen not to blame me for the attacks on 9/11, it appeared not everyone agreed with their assessment. Many believed that just by sharing the same faith, I shared the burden of the guilt and blame as well. And although 9/11 was not the start of people blaming me for the crimes of others—even in high school a teacher had publicly berated me in front of the whole class about what "my people" had done in the Oklahoma City bombing (later it was revealed that Timothy McVeigh, a white man, had committed the domestic terrorist attack)—after 9/11 the uptick of such incidents rose sharply.

As the years unfolded, other tragedies took place upon American soil. Like Sandy Hook, where kids as young as my own children, loved just as dearly, were now gone because of an angry man with a gun. I read in the news about a movie theater terrorized during a Batman screening. So many lives lost—so many that would never be the same again. And I grieved for the lost, and I grieved for their parents and families and loved ones whose lives would never be whole again.

But no one looked at *me* funny for those tragedies. No one seemed to inquire after me for an apology. In fact, no one looked at *any* group for an apology for those crimes. When their crimes were reported, their religion or race did not play into the headlines.

But when the person who committed the violence had a Muslim surname, like the Orlando Pulse shooting, suddenly I not only grieved for the lost, but also had to go into defensive mode as I braced for the blame and the looks. Overnight my social media shifted from mentions about books and writing to notifications to "Go back where I came from," and other things not fit for print. Muslim American friends shared about the bullying their children were facing by other neighborhood children. Friends in hijab, their faith more visible than others, endured the brunt of name-calling and silent glares. All this because a man whom none of us knew, whose atrocity all of us were horrified by and grieved over, identified as Muslim. For this one reason we were once again put in the spotlight and looked at with suspicion. And here's a funny thing. When people blame me and shame me even when I know full well it's not my fault—a strange human part of me ends up *feeling* guilty.

And maybe you do too.

Maybe you see the latest tragedy overseas or in your own country and the person or people shared your faith, or your skin color, and maybe you're like me. You feel that horror mixed with grief everyone else is feeling, and then you feel a helplessness and growing sense of fear that people are going to blame you.

I understand. I have been there. But as someone who is a professional apologizer, I want you to know this: When a random person or people with Muslim last names commit an atrocity in London, or Turkey, or even in your city, *it is not your fault.*

Even if the media shows their prayer rugs and you think, *I have prayer rugs too.* Even if one of them wore a hijab and you think, *I wear a hijab too.* Even if they say they did it for Islam and you think, *I am Muslim too.* I'm going to say it again: It is not your fault.

There are people who call themselves Christian and have committed unspeakable harm. They can preach about their Christian values as justification for their hateful actions all they want, but it doesn't make it so, and it certainly does not mean all Christians are to blame. That same logic applies when someone who identifies as Muslim commits a crime. You are not to blame because they say they share your faith. And you are not to blame because the media or your teacher or your classmates choose to blame you.

Would someone ask you to apologize for the kid in your biology class who ran a red light and crashed into a pole?

Would you expect the authorities to show up at your house because there was a burglary and the suspect lived in your neighborhood?

Of course not. You had nothing to do with it.

And this too is the same thing.

Muslims are not a monolith. We consist of one billion human beings. Each of us is a unique individual, and each of us is accountable for what *we as individuals* do.

It is not easy to be an American Muslim these days, and I can't promise you the future will be rosy and wonderful, because as much as I would like to, I don't know what the future holds. But I do know one thing: You can apologize for the fender bender you got into. You can apologize for the mean words that slipped out when you hadn't had your morning coffee. But you do not owe anyone an explanation or an apology for the actions of other people who happen to have Muslim surnames. Take that guilt, write it down on a piece of paper, and crumple it. Dispose of it. Yes, people may still blame you. Yes, people may still demand explanations and apologies and condemnation. But that's on them. It's not on you. There is plenty of work to do, there are plenty of mistakes you will make, but apologizing or feeling guilt for the crimes of others is not your burden to bear.

Be the best individual you can be. Let others see and hear and know you as a person accountable only for yourself. That and that alone is all you owe anyone.

HOPE NATION

DAVID LEVITHAN   LIBBA BRAY   ANGIE THOMAS

ALLY CONDIE   MARIE LU   JEFF ZENTNER

NICOLA YOON   KATE HART   GAYLE FORMAN

CHRISTINA DIAZ GONZALEZ   ATIA ABAWI

ALEX LONDON   HOWARD BRYANT   ALLY CARTER

ROMINA GARBER   RENÉE AHDIEH   AISHA SAEED

JENNY TORRES SANCHEZ   NIC STONE

JULIE MURPHY   I. W. GREGORIO   JAMES DASHNER

JASON REYNOLDS   BRENDAN KIELY

JENNY TORRES SANCHEZ

In the Past

THE EARLIEST MEMORY I HAVE of my father is running away from him. I am about three years old, and the world is tilted at an angle as I peer into my parents' bedroom and see him half dressed, stumbling around.

Then I am over my mother's shoulder and she is running. She is pulling my older sister next to us by the hand. I catch glimpses of my sister's scared face each time we pass an orange streetlight.

I don't remember what happens next. I don't remember the next day. But I remember it as the first of similar memories to come.

I spent my whole childhood and adolescence scared of my father. Scared of his voice and the scrape of his cowboy boots on the kitchen floor when he'd come home from work. His presence, the threat of him and what he *could* do, what I'd seen him do, filled me with anxiety and fear. Every moment of every day was uncertain, every movement I made had to be careful. It was impossible to know what would anger him.

One morning as I sat down for breakfast, he immediately told me to get up and go down to the basement. Because I never dared question him or defy him, I went downstairs. My father loomed behind me.

I knew I'd done something wrong, but I didn't know what it was or what I should do as we stood in the empty basement and he stared at me with strange, consuming anger. Finally, he told me I'd sat in the wrong chair. I had no idea what he meant. He looked over at an electrical cord on his workbench, and I felt my stomach drop. My mother yelled my name from the top of the stairs and demanded I get up there immediately. I didn't care if I might not make it past him, I didn't care if he might beat me or kill me for trying. I ran.

Nothing more was said about that morning. He didn't hit me ever, not that day or any day after. But my legs felt weak, like I'd escaped some terrible danger, some irreversible something.

Another time, I was nine when my dad offered to drive me to school. He told my mom not to make my lunch, that we'd stop at the deli on the way and he'd get me a sandwich. He was in a good mood. We parked and I got out from the passenger side, slamming the heavy door hard behind me, right on my finger. The door was locked, but because I was afraid of him, afraid of getting in trouble for doing something stupid and ruining the moment, I didn't say anything. I jerked my hand harshly from the door and followed my dad into the deli, hiding my hand behind me.

After a while, I felt dizzy. I tried to pay attention to what the guy at the counter was asking me, but I couldn't make sense of it. My dad finally looked down at me. *What's wrong with you?* I slowly lifted my hand, showed him my bloody, mangled finger.

He looked stricken. Worried. He rushed me home, put cartoons on the television, unwrapped my sandwich. He kept checking on me and looked grieved each time he looked my way. For days, I stared at my mangled finger and thought only of my father's kindness. It's a wonder I didn't hurt myself regularly just to get the nice version of him.

This was what my dad was like. I never knew which version of him I would get. Even when he didn't drink, he was unpredictable. His face could hold anger one moment and tenderness the next. I didn't know what to make of him. I only knew I was afraid of him. That he was bad. And good. And he was my dad. And this was our life.

I don't know what motivated my father to move us to Florida when I was ten, or why things seemed to slowly change after that. Maybe because none of my father's friends were in Florida. And there were no more weekend parties, so there wasn't as much liquor in the house. Maybe because this house had bright white walls inside and was filled with blinding sunshine that didn't so easily hide secrets. My father was obsessed with having the light come in. Or maybe because my dad got an interstate trucking job and spent most of his time on the road, hauling produce up and down the East Coast, which gave us a little room to breathe. I don't know. It just happened.

I remember being scared when we got to Florida, of starting somewhere new, but my classmates were scared of me because I was from New York and they thought that meant I was tough. I knew fear and how it could work, so I played into their assumptions, told them lies about how many kids I'd beaten up on the playground back home. And told anyone who would listen all kinds of fantastic things about New York. Anything but the truth.

Eventually, my teacher tired of my stories and asked me one day, "What do you not miss about New York?"

I thought about it for a second.

"My house," I told her. "I don't miss my house at all."

"Your house?" She looked at me funny. "How can you *not* miss your house?"

I shrugged and ate my fruit snacks. I wasn't saying any more.

My house in New York had brown carpeting that hid every stain, and wood paneling. It was dark inside, and it held our secrets. It held violence. It held too much liquor. It held the smell of hangovers and the view of my father's car parked across our front lawn for all the neighbors to see, the door left wide open overnight. My house held my father and his anger.

I spent summer vacations after we moved visiting and hanging out with cousins in New York. And later, when my sister got married, I spent them with her in New Jersey. The way I traveled was to catch a ride with my father in his eighteen-wheeler. I liked these trips, despite the awkwardness between my father and me. He wasn't exactly the person he used to be, but this somehow made it harder to know who he really was. We'd stop at Waffle Houses and eat silently across from each other. I never knew what to say to him. Sometimes what I wanted was to just ask him why. Why had he been the way he had been? But I didn't have the courage then to be so direct with him, to bring up anything from the past, so we'd get back on the road. And I'd stare out the window and watch the cars below pass me by as I wondered about the people inside. I'd watch them cut my father off and hear him curse up a storm as tiny tree air fresheners spun around wildly. I'd listen to the gruff voices on the CB radio and try to figure out what they were saying. I'd fixate on the blurry white dashes on the road.

When we did talk, he'd ask about school, or soccer, or general things. Sometimes, we'd find ourselves mentioning something about New York, but he never brought up the things I remembered. Never admitted my memories were real. I wondered if he was pretending they didn't happen, or if he really didn't remember they had. In the twilight, when he couldn't really see my face, I'd look over and study his profile as he stared at the road ahead and I'd wonder who my father was. Sometimes when we ran out of words, he'd pop in a tape to cover up any silence, and we'd listen to *rancheras*—songs about people done wrong.

It wasn't until my later teen years that I realized the extent of abuse my father had suffered as a kid, that some of the stories he'd told in a joking manner were partial confessions of a far worse reality. He began filling in the truths of those stories on those trips as I got older. He talked more about his life in Santa Rosa, and I learned of the things he had endured, that his mother had endured as a child as well. He never called it abuse, but that's what it was. He'd get pensive and say it was just the way things were back then. I wish I had told him no, not everyone was treated the way he was. I wish I had told him he should have been loved more, better. That he didn't deserve any of what he experienced. I didn't say those things to him then because maybe I didn't really know them yet. And I still had not found my voice for those kinds of conversations. All I could do was swallow my sadness as I pictured my father as a scared child.

Those road trips with my father stayed with me through the years as our family changed. I used to close my eyes at night and picture him on the road. I wondered what filled his mind all those hours he spent driving, if he ever thought about those years in our old house or our life in New York or me and my sister scared. If he ever understood or knew the extent of our fear. I wondered what he would think if he knew that for years I dreamed of loose lions and bears in our house. Last Christmas, the time of year that long ago always began well enough but always ended violently, with yelling and screaming, crying, or a fist through a wall, my father looked at my sister and me and choked out an apology. For the fear and the memories he had created and for the ones he wished he had created instead.

I could not find the words. I did not want, could not stand, for him to hurt. He'd transformed so much over the years, I felt like the man before me was not the same one who had existed then. He's become a gentle man. One who worries about people forgotten and disposed, who sees the humanity in people others are afraid to approach. My sister and I looked at each other, fumbled with our responses, and fell back to the way we'd always handled things with my father. We covered up our feelings, pretended it was no big deal. *Forget it*, we told him. *We never think of it*. He looked at us like there was more he needed to say, like he needed us to say more, too, but we couldn't hear any more, couldn't say any more. *Forget it*, we insisted.

I went home that night and cried. I went to sleep remembering my road trips with my father and the smell of diesel. And I wondered if the highway he's driven all these years is littered with his demons.

I don't know why or how things worked out the way they did with my dad. But because of him, I have an unshakable belief that things *can* get better. It's the truest thing I can tell you. In the darkest, scariest moments of my life, I could not have known things would be okay. I could not have believed my father could one day be a man unafraid to cry, who wouldn't touch hard liquor, who I wouldn't be afraid of. But he is.

I've lost hope in people and the world many times. Hope is something I think you lose and find many times in life. And I know things could have gone a very different way with my father. But they went this way. And it's why I know hope exists. Because there was nothing I wanted more when I was younger than to not be that scared little kid in that dark house anymore. There was nothing I wanted more than for the person I feared so much to be someone different. There was nothing I wanted more than to know what to do with all the feelings and secrets I kept bottled up for all those years.

So here I am, writing to you, telling you to trust and hope and believe.

DAVID LEVITHAN   LIBBA BRAY   ANGIE THOMAS
ALLY CONDIE   MARIE LU   JEFF ZENTNER
NICOLA YOON   KATE HART   GAYLE FORMAN
CHRISTINA DIAZ GONZALEZ   ATIA ABAWI
ALEX LONDON   HOWARD BRYANT   ALLY CARTER
ROMINA GARBER   RENÉE AHDIEH   AISHA SAEED
JENNY TORRES SANCHEZ   **NIC STONE**
JULIE MURPHY   I. W. GREGORIO   JAMES DASHNER
JASON REYNOLDS   BRENDAN KIELY

NIC STONE

Always

SO [SPOILER ALERT]: FOR MY entire life—as in *since birth*—I've been African American.

Most of the time, it's not a Big Deal, and I hardly notice. I move through my days like I assume a lot of people do: waking up, getting dressed, eating, doing all the stuff I *have* to do (#responsibilities), chores, showering, sleeping at night . . . And on.

And on.

And on.

But.

Sometimes it *has* felt like a Big Deal. And I *do* notice.

There was the time in fifth grade when, a few months after moving to a new state and school, I was tested for placement in the Gifted program (do they still call it that?) and became one of two spots of brown on the pale-skinned landscape of our elementary school's Focus and Challenge Math classes.

There was the time in sixth grade when, upon discovering my love of Alanis Morissette and No Doubt—Gwen Stefani's old band—another African American kid looked at me and said "Man, you a

Oreo." (That's "black on the outside, white on the inside," for the uninitiated. And it's *not* a compliment.)

There was *To Kill a Mockingbird*, *Of Mice and Men*, and *The Adventures of Tom Sawyer*, all required reading at some point in my Gifted language arts classes where I was either the *only* African American kid or one of two—a position that made reading these books in particular (one about a wrongfully accused [then murdered] black man who gets no justice, one with the n-word tossed around like a Frisbee, and one where the one black character with a speaking role is an escaped slave whom I couldn't understand half the time) more than a little uncomfortable.

There was the time senior year when a girl in one of my classes, where I was the only African American, thought I was lying when I told her my ACT score because it was two points higher than hers. Why she was shocked, I have no idea. But it definitely made me look around and take note of my African Americanness.

There was even a time when I *didn't* notice until later: I was nineteen and on a road trip with one of my friends—also African American—and while cruising through middle-of-nowhere Illinois, we got pulled over. The officer made my friend sit inside his cruiser while he ran her license and registration. Then after a few minutes, he walked her back to the car, returned her stuff, and told her to take her graduation tassel down from the rearview mirror. "It's illegal to have anything hanging up there," he said. And that was it. No ticket given. We hadn't been speeding. Neither of us had a clue why he pulled us over.

Except now, maybe we do know. I can only speculate, obviously, but bottom line: Thinking about that experience makes me feel like my African Americanness might have been a Big Deal then.

It makes me notice it.

And that was thirteen years ago. Which is interesting because I find that nowadays, I notice my African Americanness more and more instead of less and less, like I would've expected to as we **progress** through time. As a matter of fact, ever since November 8, 2016, it feels like a Big-Deal-More-Often-Than-Not.

Don't get me wrong: There were many moments before that date—over the preceding four years, especially—when the Big Deal feeling was in full effect. Like every time the name of an African American was preceded by the "#" symbol on Twitstagrumblrbook (or *social media*, as we oldies say) because another black person had been killed by police. Or every time I heard a racial slur or "joke" aimed at President Barack Obama.

Overall, though, it was fine. I felt at ease. Unfettered. The world was spinning, and I was happy with my place in it.

Even during the lead-up to November 8, 2016—that year-or-so-long campaigning and preelection debate season—I was cool. Chillin'. Were there some instances of people saying and doing things that would've normally made me notice my African Americanness? Of course.

But it was fine, because I didn't think *those people* would win.

Why would I have? There was an African American man behind the desk in the Oval Office. People of *all* races were getting angry about the abrupt ends to certain African American lives at the hands of individuals paid to *protect and serve*. African American friends and family members were going to medical school, buying homes, touring private schools for their kids. And not only did the highest-paid athletes and entertainers have skin the same color as mine, but so did everyone's favorite astrophysicist (lookin' at you, Neil deGrasse Tyson).

I'd even gotten a book deal. A chance at fulfilling my biggest dreams.

The African Americanness wasn't a burden. It really wasn't anything at all. Just a fact of life. A biological reality.

No Big Deal.

I hardly ever noticed it at all.

But then November 8, 2016, happened.

And when I woke up on November 9, the brown of my skin was all I could see.

What the results of the 2016 presidential election said to me personally was *You are not safe. There are a lot of people in this country who—consciously or not—care more about maintaining their privilege than seeing a fairer society. Enough of them, in fact, to elect a candidate whose policies will clearly have a negative impact on most marginalized communities.*

It said to me, *Your skin color is a Big Deal.*

For months, every time I saw a white person, I wondered what they thought of me as an African American. Did *they* notice the brown of my skin? (*How could they not?* was always the follow-up question.) Were they disdainful of my presence and progress? Did they feel like the America where things were more equitable for me wasn't as **Great** as the America where marginalized folks—like me—were more or less confined to the sidelines?

I was angry. I was afraid.

I was uncomfortable going to Stone Mountain, one of my favorite places in Atlanta, because the Confederate flags at the foot of the hiking trail seemed to stand extra tall after the election. Visiting also involved seeing the mountain's Confederate Memorial: a carving larger than a football field of Jefferson Davis, Robert E. Lee, and Thomas "Stonewall" Jackson—three men so bent on keeping my ancestors enslaved, their homies seceded from the Union and then started a war over it.

I felt a deep and abiding sense of sorrow every time I saw a bumper sticker about Making America **Great** Again because I would notice my African Americanness and think, *Wow, that person hates me and wishes I weren't here.*

Hope was hard.

But I kept going. Didn't have much of a choice, really: I have two little African American dudes—my sons—who need *me* to teach them how to navigate this landscape. So I settled into the noticing. I accepted that, despite what felt like eight solid years of **progress**, being black in this country was (*is*) still a Big Deal.

But it was fine. It *had* to be fine.

So whatever. New reality. Travel bans and anti-immigration rallies and desecrations of Jewish cemeteries and threats on synagogues and Klan rallies are very real things even in this **progress**ive age. I just had to be careful. Avoid the drivers with Confederate flag stickers all over their trunks (and *man*, are there more of those than you'd expect). Stay away from the small towns where people fly Confederate flags in their front yards. Don't get gas at the exit right after a "Make America Great Again" billboard.

And when visiting little towns in the Smoky Mountains of Tennessee for a writing retreat—not too far past a clearing visible from the highway where seven massive Confederate flags wave at passersby like Miss America—be on your guard when you go to the grocery store.

And so I was.

In March 2017, a good friend and I drove from Atlanta to a town in Tennessee for a five-day, four-night writing retreat in the mountains. On the way up, we saw billboards and fields of flags that made it *clear* we were passing through places where we wouldn't be warmly welcomed.

So on the late morning we decided to hit the store, I was acutely aware of our African Americanness. It almost felt like a "Hey, look at my blackness!" homing device.

And people were nice enough—lots of smiles and an offer of assistance when I struggled to find the fruit snack aisle. (Why else would one go to the grocery store while on retreat in the Smoky Mountains?) My friend even bought some Girl Scout cookies from a young lady and her father who were selling them out front—but I was still wary.

This wariness increased when we returned to our rental car and saw the pickup truck in the parking space across from ours. There was a white guy behind the wheel, smoking a cigarette with an arm draped out the open window. He was youngish (probably mid-to-late twenties). Kinda gruff looking (but a little bit cute too).

And he was staring at us. Watching with narrowed eyes.

I'd be lying if I said I wasn't utterly terrified.

But.

I also try to live by the mantra *Kill 'em with kindness.*

So, I decided to try to defuse the tension I was feeling. Looking back, it was a pretty stupid move. (Who tries to "kill someone with kindness" in the face of imminent danger? It's like telling a guy with a gun to your head that you like his shoes.) But I had to say *something*. Because even after we'd gotten into the car, he was still staring. Hard.

So I locked eyes with him and smiled. Then I rolled down my window and stuck my head out: "You look like Chad Michael Murray," I said.

He lifted his chin in acknowledgment.

I got scared-er.

So scared, I froze. Couldn't get my eyes to disconnect from his.

His eyes narrowed a little more . . .

And then he grinned. "I like your sweatshirt," he said.

And then the world exhaled. The clouds parted and the sun broke free. I looked at my friend, and we both started laughing.

That sweatshirt I was wearing? It said "Straight Outta Azkaban."

I told the guy thanks and to have a nice day, and he nodded and said, "Y'all too."

And I drove away from that grocery store with a completely different outlook. Because despite our obvious dissimilarities, this guy clearly liked something I love.

I've been a die-hard Potterhead since *Prisoner of Azkaban* (the book) came out a couple of weeks into my freshman year of high school. *Sorcerer's Stone* and *Chamber of Secrets* were both brilliant, of course, but *Prisoner of Azkaban* did something for me that the other two didn't, because it was the first time I got a grip on how truly *alone* Harry was.

From his trip on the Knight Bus to his weeks alone in the Leaky Cauldron to his discovery of the speculation that some deranged lunatic (who'd escaped from a place said to be inescapable) was after *him*, the depth of Harry's isolation—his existence in a place literally *no one else* could get to, let alone understand—crawled down inside me and curled up tight.

Because at that point in my life, I was feeling pretty alone too. But Harry was more alone than I could ever be. And knowing that helped me keep my own head above water.

It gave me **hope** that things could get better.

After that, I was done for. I devoured *Goblet of Fire* when it came out the next year. I got my first Hogwarts poster and hung it over my bed. I got an amazing Potter throw blanket that, like a little kid with her favorite teddy bear, I took with me everywhere—friends' houses for sleepovers, faraway cheerleading competitions, student council retreats, spring break road trips to the beach, you name it.

I'd just graduated from high school when *Order of the Phoenix* came out, but I wasn't *too cool* to wrangle a couple of friends into joining me for the midnight release party at our local Barnes & Noble.

Wearing witches' hats, of course.

Heck, I'm in my early thirties now, and though I tell people we're listening to the Potter audiobooks in the car to keep the kids engaged during our commute, I'm totally lying. Those audiobooks are for me.

Harry Potter—the boy, the books, the films, the *world*—is something I love to my very core. (I'm a Slytherin, by the way.)

So to hear a guy I initially took for someone who might *hurt* me say he **liked** something that represents my deep and abiding love for a Thing that's such a huge part of me?

Yeah. Utterly life changing.

The whole way back to the cabin—and ever since, really—I thought about my own thinking. My fear. My intense noticing of my African Americanness in certain situations.

The *prejudice* those things engender within me in the name of *safety*.

And don't get me wrong: It's important to stay safe, and in our present political and societal climate, the fear many marginalized folks feel is overwhelmingly valid. Within the past month of my writing this essay, another unarmed African American teen boy was killed by a police officer (rest in glory, #JordanEdwards), and two white men were stabbed to death while trying to protect a pair of Muslim girls from a third white man who was hurling racist and anti-Muslim insults at them.

The danger *is* real, and I would never, ever tell any marginalized person they shouldn't be afraid.

But what the encounter taught *me* (and maybe it'll be true for you too, dear reader) is that *my* fear of others strips them of their humanity.

Before this encounter, I would've never even *considered* that someone as different from me as Pickup Truck Guy could **like** something I like. That there would be a point of connection we could probably have a really exciting conversation about. It brought up all these questions for me: *What house could this dude be in? Would he be into the Dark Arts (my sweatshirt* does *imply that I've done time in the notorious wizarding prison)? What are his thoughts on house elfs? Did he see that twist coming at the end of* Half-Blood Prince? *Which of the Deathly Hallows would he pick if he could have one?*

Whether this guy is as rabid a fan as I am doesn't matter. The bottom line is there's *something* capable of transcending our differences.

Which means it can also transcend our fear.

That's what Potter (and, okay, pop culture in general) does for people. It transcends and then connects. It pulls the stuff that makes us human up to the surface: the power of loss and grief, the desire to love and be loved, the capacity for awe and wonder. Within the pages of those books, many of us found solace. Empowerment. Courage to dream. Harry's adventures allowed *me* to momentarily escape my circumstances and find my *self*, my *fire*, my *will to live*, even just by watching him struggle and triumph.

In vanquishing Voldemort, The Boy Who Lived genuinely saved *my* life.

Who's to say he didn't save Pickup Truck Guy's too?

June 26, 2017, marked twenty years since *Harry Potter and the Philosopher's Stone* was published in the United Kingdom, and though that makes me feel mad old, I couldn't be more grateful for the book that downright started a revolution.

I hope we can keep it going. Because at this time, in this place, we *need* sources of connection and transcendence. We need stuff that has the power to trigger a shared smile between a black girl from Atlanta and a country white boy in a pickup truck in the Smoky Mountains of Tennessee.

I need this stuff. Because—*voila!*—I'm still African American. And at this point in history, that feels like a Big Deal. So I'm thankful for that encounter. Because now, though I notice my African Americanness more often than not, when I see someone with a different skin color or gender identity, someone who might love or believe differently from me, I have *hope* because there's **always** a chance they love Harry Potter.

There's this quote in *Deathly Hallows*—"The Boy Who Lived remains a symbol of everything for which we are fighting: the triumph of good, the power of innocence, the need to keep resisting."

That's what Harry Potter is to me. Connection. Transcendence. Hope.

Always.

DAVID LEVITHAN   LIBBA BRAY   ANGIE THOMAS

ALLY CONDIE   MARIE LU   JEFF ZENTNER

NICOLA YOON   KATE HART   GAYLE FORMAN

CHRISTINA DIAZ GONZALEZ   ATIA ABAWI

ALEX LONDON   HOWARD BRYANT   ALLY CARTER

ROMINA GARBER   RENÉE AHDIEH   AISHA SAEED

JENNY TORRES SANCHEZ   NIC STONE

JULIE MURPHY   I. W. GREGORIO   JAMES DASHNER

JASON REYNOLDS   BRENDAN KIELY

JULIE MURPHY

Hoping for Home

I AM 99.99 PERCENT TEXAN. The place I call home. The .01 percent of my heart that is not belongs to the tiny state of Connecticut—which is basically the size of the entire Dallas–Fort Worth area, the city I call home.

I had lived most of my life in my grandparents' house, where my mother was also raised. That house felt like home. It smelled like home. It *was* home.

When my family moved from Connecticut to Texas, we left much behind, but the hardest thing to let go of were intangibles: the sense of closeness that comes from living within walking distance of family, and that at-times-difficult-to-define feeling of home. But because the world is big and opportunity isn't always where you wish it to be, my family made the life-altering move when I was in second grade.

I wish I could tell you the move to Texas was always a wonderful adventure. But it wasn't. There were big family events back in the Northeast we missed, from weddings to deaths. For what? The jobs my parents had taken didn't even last long enough to warrant such a drastic move. We could've gone back home to Connecticut, and at a certain point, most people would have, but we didn't. Stubborn ego runs in our blood. We were determined to find our own home in this wild new place where everything was indeed bigger. But it took time. Longer than anyone expected, in fact.

By my freshman year of high school we had moved houses fourteen times. Many of our belongings were eternally packed into the same crumbling boxes. If the electricity wasn't being shut off, it was the water. And if it was neither of those things, we were probably being evicted.

But something happened around eighth grade—we finally got into some kind of groove—and my parents were in the position to buy their own home. Our very own little slice of the world.

The weekend after we moved into our new house, which felt like a castle, I called upon my dearest friends to help me stake my claim on my brand-new bedroom. We painted the walls a harsh, unforgiving shade of red that absolutely invigorated me. My parents hated it, which meant I loved it. I was finally at home again. I felt like Goldilocks, but instead of beds, my search was for a home and my lucky number was fifteen.

For those four years of high school, I was at war with many things: my body, my sexuality, religion, society, and whatever kind of future I hoped to have. But one thing I took comfort in was our home and my bright red room. For a while, our lives were calm. For so long, we'd only survived, but somehow we began to thrive. Or so I'd thought.

I should've seen it coming. The stacks of unopened bills with URGENT stamped on the envelopes. The unattended home repairs.

The moments when I would jump to answer the phone, but my mother would quickly shoo me away, telling me to ignore it.

Instead of paying attention to all the different clues, my sights were set on what was next. It was my senior year, and I had big dreams for life after high school. I was going to move to LA with my best friend and head to fashion school, where I knew I would turn into a fashion game changer for plus-size people everywhere.

I'd spent most of high school as a total theater nerd despite being relegated to forever playing everyone's grandma. (All my other fat theater girls know what I'm talking about. The curse of the fat girl! We fall in love too, ya know! We can even save the world if we feel like it. Alas, another essay for another day.) Many things came from my love of theater, but I was most drawn to costuming. Something about clothing spoke to me. As a fat girl, I've found that most people have already decided exactly what they think about me before I have a chance to even utter a word. Clothing always felt like the best way to subvert that—to show people who I was before the world could make that decision for me. So, yeah, the future was too exciting for me to be bothered with the present.

And then one day, I came home from school to find both my parents home from work and waiting for me with a pile of moving boxes. Foreclosure. Our home, my bright red room included, had gone into foreclosure. Neither of them said the word out loud, but we were moving because the bank was kicking us out. There were only two days before my high school graduation, and suddenly nothing felt guaranteed.

Not only were we losing our home, but I was also preparing to say goodbye to all my friends and the security blanket high school had provided. That big move to California in pursuit of fashion school? It was 100 percent off the table. If you can't pay bills, you definitely can't afford overpriced art school.

During the weeks and months that followed, I turned off my emotions like a faucet—my own personal coping mechanism. Nothing hurts if you can't feel. Numbly, I watched my friends leave for college and whatever other adventures they were setting out for. My only great adventure was to the mall, where I worked for many years while my family tried to bounce back from financial ruin.

As I grew older, I learned that for my parents, buying that house had been a big gamble that they'd unfortunately lost. I spent a long time feeling angry with them for giving me this false sense of security. But in the end, nothing about our home with my bright red room was false. My parents never gave me that home with the intention of taking it away; they'd been just as desperate for a home as I was.

I don't think struggle necessarily makes you a better person. It wears you down, that's for sure, and makes you a little wiser. But I don't think you have to suffer to become a badass. However, losing my home gave me one invaluable thing: perspective.

After my senior year, we were back to rental house jumping, flickering lights, repossessed cars, and eviction notices. I didn't pack up my bright red room and have this wonderful revelation about how fate had turned this into a positive experience with an unexpected happily ever after. Instead, I watched many of my friends come and go as they made mistakes their parents could afford to fix, in places I might never afford to go to.

Slowly, I found home in places I never even thought to look. My job at the mall. A tiny community college creative-writing class. Politically active and socially minded newfound friends. Online journaling communities. Hell, even MySpace. (Yes, I'm that old.)

Of course I was sorry to see my California-shaped bubble burst, but I say all this to let you know that if you're searching like I was, there will come a day when you wake up and realize that you've found home. And if you're anything like me, you'll see that it didn't happen all at once.

For me, it was a quiet and gradual thing. It didn't take traveling the world or sleeping on some random beach or paying an obscene amount of money for an education. All of those things are great and might even be life changers for you. But no matter what, even if you end up with none of those things, please know that you'll survive, and your friends—the ones who are going places and doing things—are as lost as you. They're just searching in different ways.

I think I'm still searching for home, but I'm searching for it in the same way a curator might slowly add to a collection—particularly and deliberately. Currently home is a collage of all my favorite people, places, and things. Home is a person who holds the most fragile parts of me, in the words I scatter on the page, in my cats (who sometimes like me), and in my dog (who always adores me). My home is in the family I've handpicked. Some are blood and others are pure kismet.

When I look back and think about losing my home and graduating high school all at once, the only way I know how to describe it is as a wind tunnel of shit. (Yes, I know. I'm very articulate.) But something I figured out along the way is that you don't always just have to grin and bear it. Sometimes you just have to survive. Sometimes you have to search for tiny hopes until tiny hopes make bigger hopes. Maybe it's a job at the mall or a pen pal or a tweet or a cat or a favorite scarf. Whatever tiny hopes you have, let them do their work on you. Let them be the hope that carries you when nothing else will.

HOPE NATION

DAVID LEVITHAN   LIBBA BRAY   ANGIE THOMAS

ALLY CONDIE   MARIE LU   JEFF ZENTNER

NICOLA YOON   KATE HART   GAYLE FORMAN

CHRISTINA DIAZ GONZALEZ   ATIA ABAWI

ALEX LONDON   HOWARD BRYANT   ALLY CARTER

ROMINA GARBER   RENÉE AHDIEH   AISHA SAEED

JENNY TORRES SANCHEZ   NIC STONE

JULIE MURPHY   **I. W. GREGORIO**   JAMES DASHNER

JASON REYNOLDS   BRENDAN KIELY

I. W. GREGORIO

Caution: This Hope Is NSFW
(but it shouldn't be)

IF ASKED TO IMAGINE THE origin story of a female urologist, most people probably wouldn't picture someone who couldn't say the word *penis* in public without blushing until her early twenties, or a girl who was so embarrassed about her body that she didn't wear skin-tight shirts until college.

And yet here I am: The kid who changed her gym clothes in a bathroom stall through junior high is now someone who examines people's privates on a daily basis. I spend thousands of hours a year talking about urinary incontinence, vaginal prolapse (look it up), erectile dysfunction, and premature ejaculation . . . with relatively more acceptable topics of dinner conversation such as cancer and kidney stones thrown in here and there.

In other words, I am 100 percent certain that Teen Me would have died of mortification if she'd known what her adult self would be up to. *Modest* is probably too tame a word with which to tag my younger self; *repressed* is more like it, but it doesn't truly capture how my issues weren't just about sex. They were about body image, gender-specific shame, and cultural boundaries.

How did a body-shy teenager end up working in the most risque specialty in medicine? It's been a long road, one that I wouldn't wish on anyone. But as I raise my young kids, I have hope that they can be spared my hang-ups. All I can do is try my hardest to break the taboos that surround our bodies. All I can do is keep trying to talk about subjects that aren't initially comfortable, so future conversations won't be quite so awkward.

I'll continue to speak loudly, even as educators and parents have intense debates about what's "appropriate" for what age.

It could save lives. I'll show you how.

I was nine years old when I first felt that my body was not my friend.

My breasts had just started to grow in, and my grandmother had already impressed upon me that they were a source of shame.

"That shirt too tight. People think you bad girl!" she scolded, and thus began a progression of ever baggier T-shirts. In my defense, it was the eighties. But there isn't a single picture of me in my early teens where I didn't have the silhouette of a cereal box. I'd also patented a bust-reducing slouch, which could be differentiated from my book-reading slouch only by the tilt of my shoulders.

Looking back, it's hard for me to pinpoint what my grandmother's fears were. She raised me after my parents divorced, and she was clearly of a different generation. Was she afraid that I would be targeted, sexualized, or objectified? Was she afraid of what the appearance of my breasts signified to others about the type of person or student I was? Or was she actually afraid my clothes would be able to exert a subliminal influence on my character through a kind of Insta-Slut Mojo?

Either way, her objections stuck, along with all the other subtle reminders that good girls do not emphasize the things that make them feminine: I basically wore sports bras for most of my teenage years. My family never went swimming, and you can bet that I never went to school dances. I wore pants during the summer, except for the occasional knee-length skort when it was really hot. When I graduated from junior high school, I wore a dress that looked like it could have come out of *Little House on the Prairie.*

I should add that I never got the birds-and-the-bees talk, aside from health class and a very insightful kids' biology book that my dad got me in fourth grade. Five years later, my best friend dressed up like a French maid for Halloween; I literally dressed up in a burlap sack (as a gravestone).

It wasn't until I was sixteen that I realized my body was a source of power.

It was the first summer since puberty that I'd spent with my mother in Taiwan, and I was finally old enough to appreciate the joys of shopping. For much of my life, I'd lived on hand-me-downs from my aunt, who was more than a decade older than me. Let's just say my style was a little bit . . . dated.

That trip to visit my mom changed everything. That was the year I fell in love with sundresses, the summer I got my first shorts that would fail a school dress code. My mother took one look at my bust-reducing slouch and grabbed me by the shoulders to force my chest out. "*Ting xiong yi-dian,*" she'd say. Stand up straight.

She also took me swimming a dozen times. The first day, I wore my towel until the minute I stepped into the pool and put it back on the second I stepped out. After each swimming trip, though,

I relied on my towel less and less. I started to relish the lingering glances I would notice from some of the teenage boys. Boys in America never looked at me like that. It may have had something to do with burlap sacks.

I couldn't exactly put my finger on it at the time, but part of my newfound ease with myself probably had to do with the fact that I was finally in a place where being Asian was the default, rather than an oddity. For the first two decades of my life, I detested my hair. I wished I were blond, or redheaded like Anne of Green Gables, and that I had locks that held a curl instead of wilting into limp, anemic waves. I hated that my friends teased me that I looked like I was squinting in all my class photos. Living for a month in a place where straight black hair and brown eyes were the standard of beauty changed the way I perceived my potential (and I was finally able to find a foundation to match my skin tone).

If this sounds a bit like that eye-rolling part of a teen movie when the ugly duckling removes her glasses and lets down her ponytail to finally become the babe she truly is, well, you're kind of right. That summer with my mom gave me license to be proud of my boobs and legs, and the amount of attention I got definitely rose exponentially in the next few years.

So did my anxiety.

Even as I became more aware of my body's potential, I became aware of its limits. Suddenly, I was aware of beauty all around me, and I cared that I could never attain it. I'd grown up with blinders on to personal appearance. This is not to say that I didn't notice when someone was objectively attractive. I had eyes, and I spent time in checkout lines ogling fashion magazines like everyone else. The difference was that when I was little, I never yearned to be one of those cover girls. It just wasn't a family value. I was never exposed to any of the fundamental knowledge required to look good. I never cared about makeup (which was expensive) or had an eye for flattering clothes (which were usually even more expensive). I knew nothing about the lengths to which people would go to style their hair (my grandmother usually cut mine) or to remove it. I still remember looking at one of my college friend's photo albums and exclaiming, "You have your mother's eyebrows," only to have her raise those very perfectly shaped arches and say, kindly, "Actually, I pluck my brows." The revelation.

Looking good is, after all, quite often a pain in the butt. It is also not very tasty. Objectively, as a doctor, I am totally on board with the idea of healthy diets. I recognize intellectually the importance of low cholesterol and good glycemic control, as does anyone who's ever had to cut through the plaque-filled arteries of a man with heart disease or treated a dialysis patient whose kidneys failed because of diabetes. But food—good, savory, decadent, artfully prepared food—has always been my siren call. Like a wise person once said, some people eat to live, others live to eat.

Guess which one I am? And guess whose mother doesn't particularly approve of this philosophy?

On the very day that I wrote this paragraph, my mother sent me an email reminding me to exercise regularly and eat more vegetables. *PIGU TAI DA, BU HAO KAN,* she wrote in all caps. That's basically Chinese for "You've got a potbelly. You look awful."

It didn't take me too long after my ugly duckling moment to realize that any source of power can be used both for and against you.

We live in a world where beauty is currency, where certain bodies are perceived to be of greater value and others are devalued. As I became more aware of how I could increase the value of my body, I realized that sometimes I wasn't willing to pay the price.

The cost of body privilege is threefold. It can be superficial: the things you do to yourself, such as regulating what you eat (in ways both ordered and disordered), wearing high heels, submitting yourself to electrolysis, or waking up at five in the morning to participate in socially approved torture at the gym. It can be external: the things that others do to you, like staring at your cleavage, discounting your intellect because of your looks, or justifying your rape by saying that you dressed like you wanted it. And it can be internal: the self-hatred you feel when you blame yourself for your inability to stick to a diet, the jealousy that flares when you're afraid that you're not matching an arbitrary standard of beauty.

In the end, you can control your body to some extent, but you can't control how other people perceive you. Which is why oscillating between unnecessary shame and false pride, as I did for so many years, changes nothing.

It wasn't until medical school that I finally started to understand the alternative to shame or pride: acceptance.

Starting in anatomy class—where we unzipped the bags covering naked cadavers and meticulously carved apart their bodies—medical school broke down everything it means to be human. In the end, a body is just an intricately orchestrated group of cells. Nothing more, and nothing less. In an anatomy lab, where baby doctors learn to appreciate the complex mechanisms that make life possible, every body is priceless.

Early on, too, medical professionals learn that normal is a range, not a singularity. Disease doesn't discriminate against body type or facial symmetry. All bodies are, in the end, equal.

This detachment that doctors must use when treating patients can be baffling to people not in the medical field. In the case of urology, the ability to maintain a clinical distance can be shocking even to other physicians. One of my medical school friends once asked me how I can keep a straight face when I ask a patient about, say, premature ejaculation (protip: It's treatable with antidepressants like Zoloft). The easiest way I can explain how mundane it's become to examine a guy's private parts is to compare it to the way a new parent's perspective on breasts changes when a mom nurses their baby.

For many new moms, exhausted, engorged with milk, and with a baby wailing like a siren in arms, the sense of propriety that leads women to hide their boobs from prying eyes goes out the window. For many dads, watching their exhausted, engorged wives whip out their mammary glands while a baby wails like a siren in their arms is as sexy as watching a cow get milked. Honestly, they probably get more aroused by the instant silence when a baby latches on to a nipple than anything else.

New moms, like doctors, are just doing their job with the body parts they're given.

At its worst, clinical distance can make people feel like they're cars in for a tune-up. They can feel objectified in the worst possible way, treated like meat rather than as people. But at its best, medical perspective is liberating. The best doctors manage patients at their most vulnerable by giving them the knowledge that their source of embarrassment, whether it be their weight or their pubic hair, their breasts or their anuses, their penises or their vaginas, is nothing to be ashamed of.

Countless studies have shown that body shame keeps patients from seeking medical care time and time again. Overweight patients, who are *already* more likely to feel uncomfortable with their bodies, often put off regular checkups because they know they'll be chastised and fat-shamed. Studies show that transgender people avoid seeing doctors out of fear of the judgment of medical professionals. Earlier this year, I treated a young man who noticed one day that there was a lump in his testicle. He did nothing for six months before another doctor was finally able to persuade him to see a specialist.

As a urologist, I see one or two men a month who refuse rectal exams because of embarrassment or fear of discomfort. The potential health problem that lack of screening causes is so dangerous that the Pennsylvania Urologic Association created a campaign for prostate cancer awareness called "Don't Fear the Finger." I have a giant blue foam finger—the kind people wave at baseball games—as proof of the prevalence of male discomfort with anal penetration. (I'll bet the copyeditors for this anthology never thought that'd be something they'd have to proofread.)

And as someone on the other side of the exam table, I get it. Despite my years of training, even though I've quite literally seen it all, I sometimes struggle to defuse a patient's embarrassment. When in doubt, I use humor, taking the cue from one of my senior attendings during residency, who used to distract men during their vasectomies by telling dirty jokes. I console patients with observations like,

"Well, I can guarantee you that I've got the smallest fingers in my practice" (all of my colleagues are guys) and smile ruefully when I tell women with incontinence that they can blame it on their kids. I look people in the eye, shake their hands firmly, hoping through my body language to say, "There's nothing to be embarrassed about. Just another day at the office."

Even still, I make mistakes. Once in a while a joke lands like a lead balloon, or I'm running late so the exam seems rushed or cursory. Once a male patient joked, "That's it? You didn't even take me out to dinner." The first time I treated a patient who was intersex (a biological condition in which a person has sex characteristics that fall outside of traditional conceptions of "male" or "female"), I stumbled over the words to use to explain that her vagina was shorter than average but could be dilated. Sometimes I slip when using pronouns with a transgender patient, or bend myself into contortions trying to find the right way to refer to their genitalia.

This last lapse makes me feel exceptionally bad, because people are obsessed with what's "down there" in transgender and intersex bodies. That's the fascination, right? What's in their underwear is part of what makes it all of prurient interest, because people are uncomfortable with the idea that biology might not determine gender, after all.

The stigma associated with sex organs that don't conform to societal expectations extends to men who have had penile injuries caused by cancer or military trauma—both of these groups have significantly higher rates of depression and suicidal thoughts because of the truly toxic association of anatomy with both masculinity and femininity. Is it possible that we still live in a world where a war hero doesn't consider himself to be of any value unless he has a penis and testicles? Or where a woman is undesirable if she doesn't have breasts?

In the complex economy of the body, of course, reproductive organs are the blue chip properties, to the point that if a man is castrated, he is "unmanned," and women who are unable to bear children carry a maddening stigma to this very day. I've had a man with penile cancer tell me that he'd literally rather die than lose his penis, a high price indeed to pay for the body you want.

In a perfect society, what is under one's fig leaf wouldn't have anything to do with how a person is treated. The tricky part, of course, the underlying dominant paradigm that we're working against, is the whole issue of making babies. Sexual reproduction does currently require a sperm and an egg, and a uterus to carry the embryo in. The ability to be a good parent, however, doesn't. Neither does the ability to love. That more and more kids are growing up realizing the truth of this is one of the things that, above all, gives me hope.

After four decades on this earth, I still struggle at times to accept my body, even though at my most honest moments I understand that as an able-bodied woman of average weight and height, whose identity corresponds to her birth sex, there is very little about my body that is out of the ordinary. It's easy for me to preach body acceptance to my kids, but harder to prepare them for the hordes of people out there who fetishize or revile bodies that fall outside the arbitrary definition of "normal."

All I can do is tell them, candidly, that just because the parts of the body that their swimsuits cover are "private," it doesn't mean that they need to be ashamed—or overly proud—of those parts. Their minds and their kindness better represent their true value as people.

All I can do is educate them on the brilliance of human physiology, the mind-boggling cascades of enzymes and chemical reactions that make every body a wonder. Nowhere is this miracle more apparent than in a hospital ward, when you see so clearly that all bodies, in the end, fail.

All I can do is try to teach my children that there is no normal when it comes to being human; you can dissect a million bodies, and every one of them will be different, complex, and deserving of compassion.

It's a compassion I didn't have for myself when I was a teen, but I can hope.

DAVID LEVITHAN   LIBBA BRAY   ANGIE THOMAS

ALLY CONDIE   MARIE LU   JEFF ZENTNER

NICOLA YOON   KATE HART   GAYLE FORMAN

CHRISTINA DIAZ GONZALEZ   ATIA ABAWI

ALEX LONDON   HOWARD BRYANT   ALLY CARTER

ROMINA GARBER   RENÉE AHDIEH   AISHA SAEED

JENNY TORRES SANCHEZ   NIC STONE

JULIE MURPHY   I. W. GREGORIO   **JAMES DASHNER**

JASON REYNOLDS   BRENDAN KIELY

JAMES DASHNER

Four-Letter Words

HOPE IS A FOUR-LETTER WORD.

That's the first thing that popped into my head as I sat down to write. I'm sitting by the ocean in the city of Perth, Western Australia. For a kid who grew up in relatively (my goodness, that word, it means so much in the context of our topic) humble circumstances in a small town in Georgia, that statement seems outrageous. Australia barely registered as an actual, physical place to a kid like that—a kid whose biggest adventures in life consisted of trips to visit Grandma in South Carolina. Never, not once, did I dream that someday I might visit Australia, much less go there in the capacity of an author, to sign books for people who had been so nice as to read the stories I wrote.

But I'm here. I'm in Australia. By the Indian Ocean, an ocean that I thought might've been made up by rascally explorers after a few drinks on their rickety wooden ship. And tomorrow I'll be signing books for "fans." In Australia.

I know what this sounds like. Humble bragging. I hate humble bragging as much as you, and I'm probably guilty. But I have a point. Deep inside me, deep within the hidden compartments of a complicated human being, I have a point that I hope to make to you, the reader. And how appropriate. There's that word again. *Hope*. The four-letter beast that is ever present above us, flapping its scaly, venous, gigantic wings, daring us to take flight upon its back even as its hideous, hot breath warns us to stay away.

Hope.

Here's where I become brutally honest. I'm a white heterosexual male, raised in the good ole U.S. of A., by a family that loved me, parents who cared, in a stable home with both heat and air-conditioning. I can't remember a single time in my entire existence where I felt true hunger, despite the shameful tendency we have as relatively (that word again) stable Americans to say "I'm starving" when we've gone half a day without a solid processed meal. I've never been beaten. I've never been assaulted in any way. I've never been thrown in jail, deservingly or not. I've never been the victim of even the slightest racial discrimination, and I've surely been the beneficiary of racial preference many times without realizing it. I've never been paid less than someone else because of my gender. I've never had to deal with any kind of gender or sexual orientation discrimination.

What's my point?

My point is this: that I'm the first to admit I've had an incredibly easy life, especially when compared with the vast majority of others out there in the world. I can't pretend to understand things that I don't understand. I haven't been in the shoes of many of you. I can't ever bring myself to utter the words "I understand." Because I don't. Life is so sickeningly unfair and I often wonder why—even feel shame about—the fact that I was born into the "easy" life. But I was. And I do *try* to understand. This I can say with complete honesty. Since becoming published, I've become friends with a much more diverse group of people, and I've met thousands of readers from all over the world. I've learned and grown tremendously as a person from these encounters, and my view of life and all its inherent cruelties has changed completely.

But again, what is my *point*? Really?

Let me keep trying to make one. Stay with me.

It's hope. I called it a four-letter word, but I didn't say it was bad. Hope is the one thing that life is about, in my opinion. Hope for a better world, hope for a better humanity, hope for a life in which each and every single person is accepted and loved, with absolutely zero exceptions. Hope for the end of hunger, the end of thirst, the end of abuse. Not for the end of pain—because hey, buddy, the world will always have pain—but the end of *unnecessary* pain. Pain that's inflicted merely by *where* you're born and the stuff of which you're made.

When I was a kid, I didn't really hear about any of this heavy stuff, much less understand it (and this was long before the age of social media, through which my own children *do* know about these issues). I was a kid, for crying out loud. A simple little kid who thought about simple things. I loved baseball. I loved movies. I loved going out in the woods and pretending to be things I wasn't, acting out entire stories, getting them out of my head and into the world— even if they were seen only by me and the animals lurking in the trees and under the bushes and pine straw. I was a nerd, a dork, a dweeb. A big fella named Ian pushed me into the urinals at school. Another kid, with unnaturally large shoulder muscles and a mullet the likes of which any eighties hair band would've died for, said mean things to me every day for no reason I can think of other than that he randomly chose me to verbally abuse and not someone else.

I liked girls who didn't like me back. I rooted for teams that didn't win. I wanted to buy shoes and jeans that my parents couldn't afford. I had a classmate who received a brand-new Corvette when he turned sixteen, as spoiled as any child I've ever known. I think I got a new shirt. In the compact world of my kid-hood, I was jealous of him. I had no capacity to understand that I should just be grateful I had clean, fresh water coming bountifully out of taps whenever I expended the small effort of turning a silvery, fingerprint-smeared knob. That I had food. That I had shelter. That I had family. That I was getting an education.

A wise therapist might ask of me, "How does this make you feel?"

It makes me feel like a tornado. A swirling, spinning jumble of thoughts and feelings that only serve to confuse my simple mind and heart. I feel in equal parts lucky and guilty. Relieved and ashamed. Smart and stupid. In some ways, the whole foundation of my existence has turned from stone to sand.

But there is one shining beacon in all of that confusion.

Hope.

I don't care who I am or what I was. What my circumstances were. Where I was born and into what I was born. I do know that at times I felt hope, and it's the one thing I felt that has not tarnished or changed or disappeared. Somewhat even beyond my own awareness, hope burned inside my chest, and it's what I held on to. Hope for what? I'm not even sure. I'm not sure I need an answer, if any of us need an answer. Hope is its own thing, its own entity, its own power. HOPE, all capital letters. As a child, I felt hope; as a newly awakened adult, I felt hope; as a middle-aged man currently, I feel hope.

There is one way in which I think I can define this elusive concept. I believe that much of my hope is made up of this ideal: that our lives take a course in which they someday serve a purpose. I honestly and truly believe that no matter your circumstances, your life experiences can someday lead to achieving a Great Purpose, caps intended, even though our own personal definitions of *Great* can vary drastically. Also, the vast, vast majority of these Great Purposes will be on an intimate level that only a few will ever understand or appreciate. But that doesn't make them any less important, any less grand in the schemes of the universe.

I think about my family, both the many who came before and the few who (so far) have come after. Not everyone is born into a loving family, but I was, and I'm eternally grateful for that. Because of this, my family is everything to me. Everything. My parents, my siblings, my grandparents, my aunts and uncles and cousins. My wife and children. They are why I exist and why I wake up every morning. Someone wise once told me that the amount you love another person is directly proportional to the amount of pain you can feel when bad things happen to them. I've had such pain.

My grandpa died when I was in high school, one of the greatest men I've ever known. Shortly thereafter, my very young cousin died in a terrible tragedy. My dad died at the age of fifty-six, and I was only twenty-five. Way too soon. My grandma passing a few years later was a toughie. There was another cousin who died as a child, and then another in her prime. These cousins might as well have been siblings, we were so close.

Death. I'm not unique in having to attend so many funerals, and I know that. But in my life, death has been the biggest source of pain I can imagine (other than a very personal story that is far too intimate to share in this essay). I hate death, and I want someone to hurry up and figure out that whole immortality thing I've been reading about in science fiction books my whole life. Come on, Stephen Hawking, Elon Musk, Neil deGrasse Tyson—anyone, get on it!

But death is a funny thing. Not ha-ha slap-your-knee funny (though sometimes pain can make us do outrageous, inexplicable things), but the kind of funny that means unexpected consequences. With each of the deaths mentioned above, I felt an incredible closeness to those who'd passed and those who were still sticking around. As spiritual an experience as I could ever describe. A power that burned inside me, matching the pain stroke for stroke. And that power was some magical combination of love and hope. As odd as it sounds, the funerals I've attended for these dear people have been among the highlights of my life, memories more precious than all the gold and silver in the world. We had no choice but to do it and to hurt from it. But paying our respects, sharing stories, remembering, being together, united in pain . . . I always left a better person than I had been when I arrived.

Family is about hope. Family *is* hope. I honestly don't have the slightest clue if that's true for everyone (though I suspect it is), but it's true for me, and no essay on the subject could omit them. I have four kids, and all the hope and love that has been bequeathed to me must go to them. They really are the most important, if not sole, purpose of my life now. My success as an author means absolutely nothing if I fail as a parent.

But it doesn't have to be an either/or situation, does it? Because the second thing that really popped into my head when I thought about this subject was my readers. The amount of hope and friendship I've derived from them is beyond measurement. It's been such a great two-way street, a mutually beneficial relationship that I'm grateful for each and every day. I wrote a few stories that allow them to escape the hardships and drudgeries of life for snippets of time here and there, and they provide me with a constant, steady flow of inspiring tales and laugh-out-loud comments. What a fantastically pleasant surprise this two-way street has been for me.

I've always wanted to be a writer. But as a snotty-nosed kid it was more like a pipe dream, like wishing to be an NFL quarterback or an astronaut. Possible, surely, but very unlikely. When I doubled down and got serious in college with my writing, I had some delusions of grandeur (as Han Solo would say). I thought I had to create a masterpiece, something "important," a book that would win every award and get me an open invitation to Oprah's house. That didn't work so well for me. It's not who I am. I finally went with what I love to read myself and wrote things like *The Maze Runner*, action and mystery and science fiction. I thought to myself (and I'm not kidding here), *Oh well, I'll never be an "important" writer and change any lives, but I'm having a lot of fun.*

It shames me how completely I underestimated the power of storytelling, especially after living an entire childhood in which storytelling affected my life more profoundly than anything else. Getting lost in a story, any story, *does* change a person. It binds us to characters, makes us feel their emotions and see our own life through a different lens, prepares us for things we may not see coming. Perhaps more than anything else, it simply allows us to escape to another world when our own is too difficult to face for a moment. Maybe many moments.

And these are the stories I've heard from readers, stories that have buoyed up my life in countless ways. One new friend had cancer and bonded with one of my characters, pulled from their strength on the page, to get through the terrifying treatments. Others have been bullied or had emotional problems or a mental illness or contemplated suicide and found a safe haven within another world, those created by myself and by many of my author friends. We swap these tales and feel uplifted and enlightened, humbled and inspired. I can say with complete honesty that my readers out there have touched me in much greater ways than I've ever touched them.

What does that sound like to me? That sounds like hope. HOPE, all caps.

So again, even now, I'm asking this question: What *is* my point? I admit this essay has mostly been a stream of consciousness, done purposefully without much planning. (Hey, knock it off. I know you're laughing and saying, *Yeah, we can tell.*) I was asked to write about hope, and I did so, trying my best to transfer my thoughts onto the page, translate the things that four-letter word ignited within my mind.

I guess this is how I would sum it up: I'm so self-conscious about living what most would view as a privileged life (again, white heterosexual male raised by a humble but financially stable family) that I became uncertain about whether I was allowed to feel hope. I thought feeling hope might even come across as an insult to those living much harder lives than I do. How dare I talk about hope when

I live a nice, neat little life inside my nice, neat little shell. And in many ways, that assessment is correct, and I'm guilty as charged. When there are countless people out there hoping for water, food, or a friend who truly accepts them, the things I've hoped for seem trite and borderline offensive.

But I am who I am. I can only promise that I've done my best to "pay it forward," to help those less fortunate, and to make every stride possible to understand things I didn't as a child. But like any writer and most people, I still think I kinda suck at it and need to do much, much better. Isn't that a problem we have on any and all levels? *I suck.* There are a million ways to say it, but we all feel it.

And that's where HOPE comes in. It's one of the few things I truly believe we can all share in this world, no matter our makeup or status or place of birth. As I've shown, it makes me think of family, both past and future generations, and the strength and love I've shared with readers through my stories and travels. It makes me think of working hard to change the world, no matter how small the way in which we do it. It probably makes you think of something in your own life that I've never even thought of. But the concept is the same. And that's my sincere message—my point, perhaps—to anyone out there who might be reading this.

You are not small. You are not insignificant. You are not unworthy. (I can think of another couple of four-letter words to describe anyone who ever tries to make you think so.)

You are great. You are magnificent. You are infinitely important to this world and to the people who come across your path. You are worthy of great things. You are capable of changing as many lives as you so choose, including your own, for the better. There is literally nothing about you, not one thing under the sun, that makes you less than anyone else. If life is rotten, then go and find those people who will accept you and love you and join your quest to change the world. I promise you they're out there.

Feel hope, my friend, whatever that means to you.

Embrace it, devour it, foster it, make it grow.

Do so, and you will have touched our planet and the people who walk upon it in a way that the eons of infinite time can never erase. You'd be forgiven for thinking I went a little crazy on the cheesy train here at the end, but it's something I truly feel. Consider yourself hugged by this page of the book, with all the sincerity I can muster.

So go and HOPE the world into submission. And just make sure you have fun while doing it.

HOPE NATION

DAVID LEVITHAN LIBBA BRAY ANGIE THOMAS
ALLY CONDIE MARIE LU JEFF ZENTNER
NICOLA YOON KATE HART GAYLE FORMAN
CHRISTINA DIAZ GONZALEZ ATIA ABAWI
ALEX LONDON HOWARD BRYANT ALLY CARTER
ROMINA GARBER RENÉE AHDIEH AISHA SAEED
JENNY TORRES SANCHEZ NIC STONE
JULIE MURPHY I. W. GREGORIO JAMES DASHNER
JASON REYNOLDS BRENDAN KIELY

JASON REYNOLDS & BRENDAN KIELY

The Kids Who Stick

BRENDAN: I've been thinking about how meaningful it is that we've spent the last two years together on a continuous road trip, talking about *All American Boys* and using it as a springboard to leap into deep conversations about race and racism and how they manifest in the smallest, subtlest moments every day and in the large, institutional systems of injustice throughout our entire society. We've traveled to nearly every corner of the country together, talked to people there, young folks in particular, and listened to them tell us about their experiences with race and racism in this country. We've seen and heard so much.

JASON: And I wonder, given that we've spoken to more than forty thousand kids, teachers, and librarians, and traveled all over, if it all ended today, if we didn't travel anymore, if we didn't speak to anyone about *All American Boys* anymore, after all these kids we've met along the way, who are the ones that stick?

B: There are so many. I remember the girl in Philadelphia, where we spoke in front of one of the most diverse schools—diverse in the truest sense—of all the schools that we've been to across the country. And after our talk, there was a young black girl waiting for you in the hallway. And her question, in my mind, was a devastating one. But what I witnessed was what I think of as one of the greatest moments of hope because of what you were able to say to her. I'm curious, though, from your perspective, if you see that as a moment of hope.

J: Yeah, I mean, it's weird because I don't know if I've ever thought about it as a moment of hope until just this minute, actually. But I do think about that moment often. *All American Boys* was a new book, and we'd just begun the tour. Philadelphia was the second or third stop, and after our presentation, I remember I had gone to the bathroom. And when I came out, there you were, standing at the end of the corridor with this young lady.

I walked up to you and all you said was "She has something she wants to say. I told her to wait for you, because she wants to ask you something."

So I kneeled down, looked her in the face. I'll never forget this because of what she said to me, that small voice fluttering with a strange uncertainty.

"Mr. Jason, has there ever been a time where you just wish you could change the color of your skin? That you could be a different color—that way you won't be treated unfairly?"

Even looking back on it now, that moment, those words hold such magnitude. It was clear that this was something that was obviously very real for her. No matter how diverse her school was, this was something she believed separated her from the rest of her classmates, so much so that she felt the need to ask privately. And in that space, for me, all my mother's teachings rose to the brim. The cultural codes tethered to me seem to light up in my psyche. All the history and the legacy of what I know to be true, the things I know live in my lineage, the things I know live within my genetics. The things that live historically and continue to metastasize presently, which should not cause us—especially this child—to hang our heads in shame. They all came to the forefront.

This was an opportunity for me to pour into the beauty of who this girl is, the beauty of who we are. That the things that have happened to us and the struggles that we continue to face as people of color in America are complicated. And perhaps they make our lives a little less than easy, but they don't necessarily always make our lives less than happy. They can make our experiences difficult, but difficulty doesn't necessarily equate to sadness. And while looking in that little girl's face, what I wanted her to know was that if she were to go to her grandma's house and see Grandma singing those songs on Sunday morning, or singing those songs on Friday night when she's frying that fish, if she were to see the kids on corners in Harlem—kids that look like her—exorcising the weight of the day to only the sounds of their own handclaps (shake a load off), if she were to take a glimpse at Serena and Beyoncé and First Lady Obama, or watch how the mothers make bread from dread, and the old men broken and bent over still iron out wrinkles and put a straight blade to that brown, and walk, strut, with pride, she would know that there is never a reason for her to want to strip herself of such a beautiful, beautiful, beautiful legacy. No matter how difficult it is, no matter how misunderstood we are. Hope is being able to look that young lady in the face and tell her she is gold, and to watch her eyes shine and her mouth curl into a smile in the moment. Then, to walk away from her, certain that I must do what I can to not let the world, and the fear it works to impose, reverse-alchemize her.

And I've seen you in these kinds of moments too. All the kids who come up to you and say, "Mr. Kiely, I'm white. And I'm afraid. What do I do?"

B: I find hope listening to the young white people who have the strength of humility. The way they enter into conversations about racism in ways that I don't often hear adults enter into them. So for example, there was that white kid whose grandfather was a police officer in New York City during the race riots in the sixties.

He walked up to me and said, "I just need to tell you this." He talked about the violence he knew his grandfather engaged in. He took a deep breath and looked me right in the eye. "Everybody tells me to remember that my grandfather was a hero. They tell me to remember that first." He was holding a paperback book, and he kept tapping it lightly in his other hand. He looked back down at the ground again until he found the words he wanted to say next. "No matter what good he did, he also did some things that were pretty terrible. I don't know why everybody else can't talk about it. I just feel like I need to or I'm living a lie."

What this kid was trying to process, the courage it took to *not* take the easy way out as friends and family encouraged him to over and over, his choice to face the truth instead, to not apologize the ugliness away by masking it in excuses—it's an honesty most white adults refuse to engage in: that the legacy of racial injustice in

America lies within all us white people today too, not as victims, but as the beneficiaries of it. His question was a powerful one.

"I don't want to be just another person not doing something about it," he said.

I shook his hand and told him how proud I was of him, how much I admired him. Then I realized he had tears pushing at the back of his eyes, so I asked him if I could give him a hug. I'm not sure who was supporting who there. He is much stronger than I was at his age, so much wiser.

There's guilt there, there's shame, and that's natural. I feel those emotions too. But I admire him because he's not letting those emotions destroy him. Instead, he's feeling them and allowing them to motivate him into action. It's a quality of leadership I admire.

I hear so many people say, "Life is unfair." Often, adults let that statement sit and resonate with philosophical weight, as if it is a condition of the universe. And while it might be, many young people have a different instinct with which they want to approach it. "Life is unfair," they say, but then they follow that immediately with, "And what can we do about it? What *are* we going to do about it?"

Many adults don't want to rock the boat. "Well, now hold on a second," they say or intimate. And as we wait, and as we go slow, time passes, and the status quo remains the same. Young people *want* to rock the boat. And we need to. Otherwise the status quo remains—and our status quo today is unconscionably unjust.

So I believe in these kids. I believe in their leadership.

I'll never forget the young black man at a school outside of DC. We were presenting in front of the whole high school, and as soon as we break into the Q and A, he stands up to ask a question. But instead of asking a question, he turns to his classmates and says something to the effect of, "If you're so enthralled with what these two guys are saying, if you think their presentation is so great, why haven't you been listening to what I've been saying in history class? Why haven't you been listening to what I have to say?" He took a minute to reiterate what he must have said before, a brief history walking the Movement for Black Lives back to SNCC [the Student Nonviolent Coordinating Committee] and other groups in the sixties.

He could have simply nodded along to what we were saying at the front of the room, remained silent, and let us speak through the megaphone that day. But instead, he grabbed the megaphone for himself and essentially said, "Do you hear me now?" He stood up to take his own leadership, and that gives me hope. Because I think he has the knowledge, he has the courage, and he has the tenacity to be a real, serious leader in our country.

Sixteen years old. What will happen? Will we listen to him?

HOPE NATION

Acknowledgments

First—there wouldn't be a *Hope Nation* without my editor and publisher, Michael Green. MG—thank you for convincing me I had time to create a book and allowing it to be THIS book. Your dedication and passion for our project have given me more hope than I deserve.

Team Hope (otherwise known as my kick-ass contributors)—thanks to each of you for allowing me to interrupt your already very busy lives and previously scheduled writing obligations. Your contributions and personal stories continue to inspire me, and I will always adore each of you for jumping right on board and digging deep to offer our readers such intimate glimpses into your pasts and present to harness hope. I'm in awe of you all, always.

Special thanks to the amazing team at Philomel and Penguin Young Readers for all the support, including Jen Loja, Emily Romero, Jennifer Dee, and especially my darlings Venessa Carson and Carmela Iaria, who remind us all that hope is indeed a decision. Same goes for my former and present posse at Penguin Random House Audio. Shout-outs to Cheryl Herman and Jodie Cohen for being so immediately enthusiastic about *Hope Nation*, and to Jen Rubbins, Dan Zitt, Katie Punia, Kristen Luby, and Heather Dalton for all their work in creating, marketing, and getting the word out about this amazing production that offers listeners a chance experience these rich stories by "reading it with their ears."

There also wouldn't be a *Hope Nation* without my goddaughter, Hannah Vance, and my niece Autumn Brock—it was your search for answers and hope in hard times that inspired this book; thank you both for being such fierce young women. Keep speaking your truths. And the other amazing young women in my life—Nicole Jordan, Daniela Villarreal, and Hillary Bellah. You are wonderful. Always be courageous.

Also, a lifetime of thanks to my niece Laticia Porter; my daddy, Marion Little; and my brothers and sisters: Ingrid Little-Kesler, James Little, and Patty and Larry Anderson, who wouldn't let the other two sibs sell me to a high or low bidder. Being the youngest can be hard, y'all. Much love to my Brock family as well. And here's to the sisters I chose for myself: Nancy Fritz Vance, Sarah Leach Burey, Laura Williams Francis, Lisa Wall Bua, and April Whatley Bedford. Love you ladies so much more than you know.

The book world has provided me with some of the very dearest friends in my life, and these pals have a hand in so much of the fun I get to experience: Ally Carter, Lizette Serrano, Dina Sherman, Gordon Korman, Elizabeth Eulberg, Carrie Ryan, Ally Condie, Sonya Sones, Sarah Mlynowski, Libba Bray, Tim Jones, Sandy London, and Varian Johnson. Thanks for always making me laugh—wishing for many more years of mischief ahead of us.

A special shout-out to all my North Texas Teen Book Festival partners-in-crime: Mandy Aguilar, Stacy Wells, Ian Pearce, Amanda Hipp, Heather Aston, Renee Newry, Amanda Trowbridge, and especially Kristin Treviño for always helping me remember that our teens come first.

For having hearts as big as our home state, my Texas posse deserves a special yee-haw, especially Nicole Caliro, Jill Bellomy, Carson Childress, Kathy Arndt, Angie Mahalik, Laila Sanguras, Missy Schliep, Monica Champagne, Victoria Tong, Stephanie Howell, Laurel Dickson, Brooke Morris, Milissa Vo, Sid Grant, Vern Edin, and Cheri Johnson, and my friends and colleagues at SHSU: Teri Lesesne, Karin Perry, Holly Weimar, Robin Moore, Elizabeth Gross, and especially Rebecca Lewis for putting a roof over my head in Huntsville. And as always, no good thing I do professionally isn't somehow tied back to my forever mentor and friend, Sylvia Vardell.

I've been so lucky to have gotten to teach and work with so many amazing teens throughout my years as an educator. Special thanks to my darlings Marcus Jauregui, Jennifer Sabatini Jabara, Chase Whale, Courtney Piano Newman, Jordan Cowen Muse, Candis Ray Morris, Samantha Kline Beltran, Lauren Lason, Courtney Cheek, and the thousands of others whose lives intersected with mine throughout the years. This book is filled with the stories I wish I could have handed you when you were a teen; I promise I was thinking of you all the while it was being created.

Finally, and most importantly, though my personal hope is inspired by so many, it's always firmly rooted in Madeleine, Olivia, and Michael, and in the legacy of my mom, Irmgard Klebe Little. All I do is in hopes of making them proud.

About the Authors

ATIA ABAWI is an award-winning foreign news correspondent and author who has lived in the Middle East and Asia for the last decade. Born a refugee in West Germany to Afghan parents who fled a brutal war, Atia was raised in the United States. Her first book for teens was the critically acclaimed and award-winning *Secret Sky*, set in contemporary Afghanistan. Her second book, *A Land of Permanent Goodbyes*, delves into the Syrian refugee crisis. She lives in Jerusalem with her husband, Conor Powell, and their son, Arian, where she covers stories unfolding in the Middle East and surrounding areas.

RENÉE AHDIEH is the author of the number one *New York Times* best seller *The Wrath and the Dawn*, *The Rose and the Dagger*, and *The Flame in the Mist*. A graduate of the University of North Carolina at Chapel Hill, Renée likes to dance salsa and collect shoes in her spare time. She is passionate about all kinds of curry, rescue dogs, and college basketball. The first few years of her life were spent in a high-rise in South Korea; consequently, Renée enjoys having her head in the clouds. She lives in Charlotte, North Carolina, with her husband and their tiny overlord of a dog.

LIBBA BRAY is the number one *New York Times* best-selling author of The Gemma Doyle Trilogy (*A Great and Terrible Beauty*, *Rebel Angels*,

The Sweet Far Thing); the Michael L. Printz Award–winning *Going Bovine*; *Beauty Queens*, a *Los Angeles Times* Book Prize finalist; and The Diviners series. She lives in Brooklyn, New York, with her family and two cats of questionable intelligence. She feels hopeful about many things, except during deadline weeks. Then it's a lot of Pink Floyd and Googling "how to fake your own death." You can find her at www.libbabray.com and on Twitter and Instagram @libbabray. You can also usually find her anyplace they serve fried chicken.

HOWARD BRYANT is a senior writer for ESPN.com and *ESPN The Magazine*. He has been the sports correspondent for National Public Radio's *Weekend Edition Saturday* since 2006 and has worked at several newspapers, including the *Boston Herald* and the *Washington Post*. A Boston native, he is the author of *Shut Out: A Story of Race and Baseball in Boston*; *Juicing the Game: Drugs, Power, and the Fight for the Soul of Major League Baseball*; *The Last Hero: A Life of Henry Aaron*; and the three-book Legends series for middle-grade readers. Mr. Bryant was a 2016 National Magazine Award finalist for commentary.

ALLY CARTER writes books for spies, thieves, and teenagers. She's the author of three *New York Times* best-selling series: The Gallagher Girls, Heist Society, and Embassy Row. Her most recent novel is *Not If I Save You First*. She lives in Oklahoma and, online, at allycarter.com.

ALLY CONDIE is the author of the Matched trilogy, a number one *New York Times* and international best seller. *Matched* was chosen as one of YALSA's 2011 Teens' Top Ten and named as one of *Publishers Weekly*'s Best Children's Books of 2010. The sequels, *Crossed* and

Reached, were also critically acclaimed and received starred reviews, and all three books are available in more than thirty languages. Her middle-grade novel, *Summerlost*, was a finalist for the 2016 Edgar Award for Best Juvenile Mystery.

JAMES DASHNER is the number one *New York Times* best-selling author of The Maze Runner series, The Mortality Doctrine series, and several other books. He lives in the Rocky Mountains with his family.

CHRISTINA DIAZ GONZALEZ is the award-winning author of several books, including *The Red Umbrella*, *A Thunderous Whisper*, *Moving Target*, and *Return Fire*. Christina's books have received numerous honors and recognitions, with publications such as *Publishers Weekly*, *the Miami Herald*, *School Library Journal*, and the *Washington Post* calling her novels engrossing, compelling, and inspirational. Christina lives in Miami, Florida, with her husband, sons, and a dog that can open doors.

GAYLE FORMAN is the award-winning, *New York Times* best-selling author of the young-adult novels *If I Stay*, *Where She Went*, the Just One series, and *I Was Here*, and of the adult novel *Leave Me*. She lives in Brooklyn, New York, with her family.

ROMINA GARBER (aka Romina Russell) is the author of the *New York Times*/international best-selling young-adult science fiction–fantasy series Zodiac. Born in Buenos Aires and raised in Miami, Romina resides in Los Angeles but would much rather be at Hogwarts. As a teen, Romina landed her first writing gig—College, She Wrote, a weekly Sunday column for the *Miami Herald* that was later picked up for national syndication—and hasn't stopped writing since. She is a graduate of Harvard College and a Virgo to the core. For more information about her books, follow her on Twitter/Instagram @rominagarber.

I. W. GREGORIO is a practicing surgeon by day, masked avenging young-adult writer by night. After earning her MD, she did her residency at Stanford, where she met the intersex patient who inspired her debut novel, *None of the Above*, which was a Lambda Literary Award Finalist, a *Publishers Weekly* Flying Start, and optioned for a TV series. She is proud to be a board member of interACT: Advocates for Intersex Youth, and is a founding member of We Need Diverse Books. Find her online at www.iwgregorio.com, and on Twitter, Tumblr, Facebook, and Instagram @iwgregorio.

KATE HART studied Spanish and history at a small liberal arts school before teaching young people their ABCs. She also wrote grants for grown-ups with disabilities and now builds tree houses for people of all ages. Her debut young-adult novel, *After the Fall*, was published in January 2017. A former contributor to YA Highway, she hosts the Badass Ladies You Should Know series, and sells woodworking and inappropriate embroidery at The Badasserie. Kate is a citizen of the Chickasaw Nation and lives with her family in northwest Arkansas.

BRENDAN KIELY is the *New York Times* best-selling author of *All American Boys* (with Jason Reynolds), *The Last True Love Story*, and *The Gospel of Winter*. His work has been published in ten languages; has received a Coretta Scott King Author Honor Award, the Walter

Dean Myers Award, and the Amelia Elizabeth Walden Award; was twice awarded Best Fiction for Young Adults (2015, 2017) by the American Library Association; and was one of the *Kirkus Reviews* Best Books of 2014. Originally from the Boston area, he lives with his wife in New York City. *Tradition* is his fourth novel.

DAVID LEVITHAN has written many young-adult novels, including *Boy Meets Boy*, *Two Boys Kissing*, *Every Day*, and *Another Day*. He's also written many collaborations, including (most recently) *Sam and Ilsa's Last Hurrah*, with Rachel Cohn. You can find out more about him at www.davidlevithan.com and find him on Twitter @loversdiction.

ALEX LONDON has written more than twenty books for children, teens, and adults, including the Wild Ones, Dog Tags, and Tides of War series for middle-grade readers. His young-adult debut, *Proxy*, has been included in numerous state reading lists, the American Library Association's Top Ten Quick Picks for Reluctant Young Adult Readers, Best Fiction for Young Adults, and the Rainbow Book List. His mom likes it too.

MARIE LU is the author of the number one *New York Times* best-selling series The Young Elites, as well as the blockbuster best-selling Legend series. She graduated from the University of Southern California and jumped into the video game industry as an artist. Now a full-time writer, she spends her spare time reading, drawing, playing games, and getting stuck in traffic. She lives in Los Angeles with one husband, one Chihuahua mix, and one Pembroke Welsh corgi.

JULIE MURPHY is the number one *New York Times* best-selling and award-winning author of *Puddin'*, *Ramona Blue*, *Dumplin'* (soon to be a major motion picture), and *Side Effects May Vary*. She lives in North Texas with her husband, who loves her; her dog, who adores her; and her cats, who tolerate her. When she's not writing, she can be found reading, traveling, watching movies so bad they're good, or hunting down the perfect slice of pizza. Before writing full-time, she held numerous jobs, such as wedding dress consultant, failed barista, and ultimately librarian. Learn more about her at www.juliemurphywrites.com.

JASON REYNOLDS is the author of the critically acclaimed *When I Was the Greatest*, for which he received the Coretta Scott King / John Steptoe Award for New Talent; the Coretta Scott King Author Honor books *The Boy in the Black Suit*, *All American Boys* (cowritten with Brendan Kiely), and *As Brave As You* (his middle-grade debut); *Patina*, and *Ghost*, a National Book Award finalist and the first in a four-book series about kids on an elite track team. Jason's most recent novel, *Long Way Down*, was long-listed for the National Book Award. Jason recently moved to Washington, DC, but before that spent many years in Brooklyn, New York, home of his protagonist in *Miles Morales: Spider-Man*.

AISHA SAEED is a founding member of We Need Diverse Books. Her novel *Written in the Stars* was listed as a best book of 2015 by Bank Street Books and a 2016 YALSA Quick Pick for Reluctant Readers. Her forthcoming middle-grade novel, *Amal Unbound*, will be published in 2018. You can follow her on Twitter @aishacs.

NIC STONE, author of *Dear Martin*, was born and raised in a suburb of Atlanta, Georgia, and the only thing she loves more than an adventure is a good story about one. After graduating from Spelman College, she worked extensively in teen mentoring and lived in Israel for a few years before returning to the United States to write full-time. Growing up with a wide range of cultures, religions, and backgrounds, Stone strives to bring these diverse voices and stories to her work. You can find her goofing off and/or fangirling over her husband and sons on most social media platforms as @getnicced.

ANGIE THOMAS was born, raised, and still resides in Jackson, Mississippi. She is a former teen rapper whose greatest accomplishment was an article about her in *Right On!* magazine with a picture included. She holds a BFA in creative writing from Belhaven University and an unofficial degree in hip-hop. She is an inaugural winner of the Walter Dean Myers Grant in 2015, awarded by We Need Diverse Books. Her debut novel, *The Hate U Give*, is a number one *New York Times* best seller and available in more than twenty countries. A film adaptation has been produced by Fox 2000, with George Tillman directing and *Hunger Games* actress Amandla Stenberg starring.

JENNY TORRES SANCHEZ is a full-time writer and former English teacher. She was born in Brooklyn, New York, but has lived on the border of two worlds her whole life. She is the author of *Because of the Sun*; *Death, Dickinson, and the Demented Life of Frenchie Garcia*; *The Downside of Being Charlie*; and her latest novel, *The Fall of Innocence*. She lives in Orlando, Florida, with her husband and children.

NICOLA YOON is the number one *New York Times* best-selling author of *Everything, Everything*, which is now a major motion picture, and *The Sun Is Also a Star*, a National Book Award finalist and Michael L. Printz Honor Boo She grew up in Jamaica and Brooklyn, and lives in Los Angeles with her family.

JEFF ZENTNER is the author of *The Serpent King*, winner of the William C. Morris, Amelia Elizabeth Walden, and International Literacy Association awards and long-listed for the Carnegie Medal. His second book, *Goodbye Days*, came out in 2017. Before becoming a writer, he was a singer-songwriter and guitarist who recorded with Iggy Pop, Nick Cave, and Debbie Harry. In addition to writing and recording his own music, he has worked with young musicians at Tennessee Teens Rock Camp, which inspired him to write for young adults. He lives in Nashville, Tennessee.

HOPE IS A DECISION.